NI MANAGEMENT DEVELOPMENT SUPER SERIES

THIRD EDITION

Managing Resources

Improving Efficiency

Published for
&NEBS Management   by   Pergamon Flexible Learning

Pergamon Flexible Learning
An imprint of Butterworth-Heinemann
Linacre House, Jordan Hill, Oxford OX2 8DP
225 Wildwood Avenue, Woburn, MA 01801-2041
A division of Reed Educational and Professional Publishing Ltd

A member of the Reed Elsevier plc group

OXFORD   AUCKLAND   BOSTON
JOHANNESBURG   MELBOURNE   NEW DELHI

First published 1986
Second edition 1991
Third edition 1997
Reprinted 1998 (twice), 1999, 2000, 2001

© NEBS Management 1986, 1991, 1997

All rights reserved. No part of this publication may be reproduced in any material form (including photocopying or storing in any medium by electronic means and whether or not transiently or incidentally to some other use of this publication) without the written permission of the copyright holder except in accordance with the provisions of the Copyright, Designs and Patents Act 1988 or under the terms of a licence issued by the Copyright Licensing Agency Ltd, 90 Tottenham Court Road, London, England W1P 0LP. Applications for the copyright holder's written permission to reproduce any part of this publication should be addressed to the publishers.

British Library Cataloguing in Publication Data
A catalogue record for this book is available from the British Library

ISBN 0 7506 3304 2

For information on all Butterworth-Heinemann publications visit our website at www.bh.com

PLANT A TREE
British Trust for Conservation Volunteers
FOR EVERY TITLE THAT WE PUBLISH, BUTTERWORTH-HEINEMANN WILL PAY FOR BTCV TO PLANT AND CARE FOR A TREE.

The views expressed in this work are those of the authors and do not necessarily reflect those of the National Examining Board for Supervision and Management or of the publisher.

NEBS Management Project Manager: Diana Thomas
Author: Joe Johnson
Editor: Diana Thomas
Series Editor: Diana Thomas
Based on previous material by: Joe Johnson
Composition by Genesis Typesetting, Rochester, Kent
Printed and bound in Great Britain

Contents

Workbook introduction — v
1. NEBS Management Super Series 3 study links — v
2. S/NVQ links — vi
3. Workbook objectives — vi
4. Activity planner — vii

Session A Background to efficiency — 1
1. Introduction — 1
2. Work organizations — 2
3. Work as a transforming process — 3
4. Introduction to resources — 4
5. Efficiency — 7
6. Why is efficiency important? — 8
7. Effectiveness — 9
8. Quality — 11
9. People as a resource — 12
10. Capital as a resource — 15
11. Materials as a resource — 18
12. Time as a resource — 19
13. **Summary** — 22

Session B Productivity and work study — 23
1. Introduction — 23
2. Productivity — 23
3. Work study — 26
4. Method study — 27
5. Selection — 29
6. Recording using process charts — 30
7. Other recording techniques — 33
8. Examination — 38
9. Development — 39
10. Definition and installation — 39
11. Maintenance — 40
12. Work measurement — 42
13. Some newer techniques — 50
14. Efficiency and effectiveness of 'white collar workers' — 53
15. **Summary** — 57

Session C Efficiency in your workplace — 59
1. Introduction — 59
2. What resources do you have? — 60
3. Planning for improved efficiency and effectiveness — 66
4. **Summary** — 74

Performance checks   75
 1 Quick quiz   75
 2 Workbook assessment   77
 3 Work-based assignment   78

Reflect and review   79
 1 Reflect and review   79
 2 Action plan   81
 3 Extensions   83
 4 Answers to self-assessment questions   84
 5 Answers to activities   87
 6 Answers to the quick quiz   89
 7 Certificate   90

Workbook introduction

1 NEBS Management Super Series 3 study links

Here are the workbook titles in each module which link with *Improving Efficiency*, should you wish to extend your study to other Super Series workbooks. There is a brief description of each workbook in the User Guide.

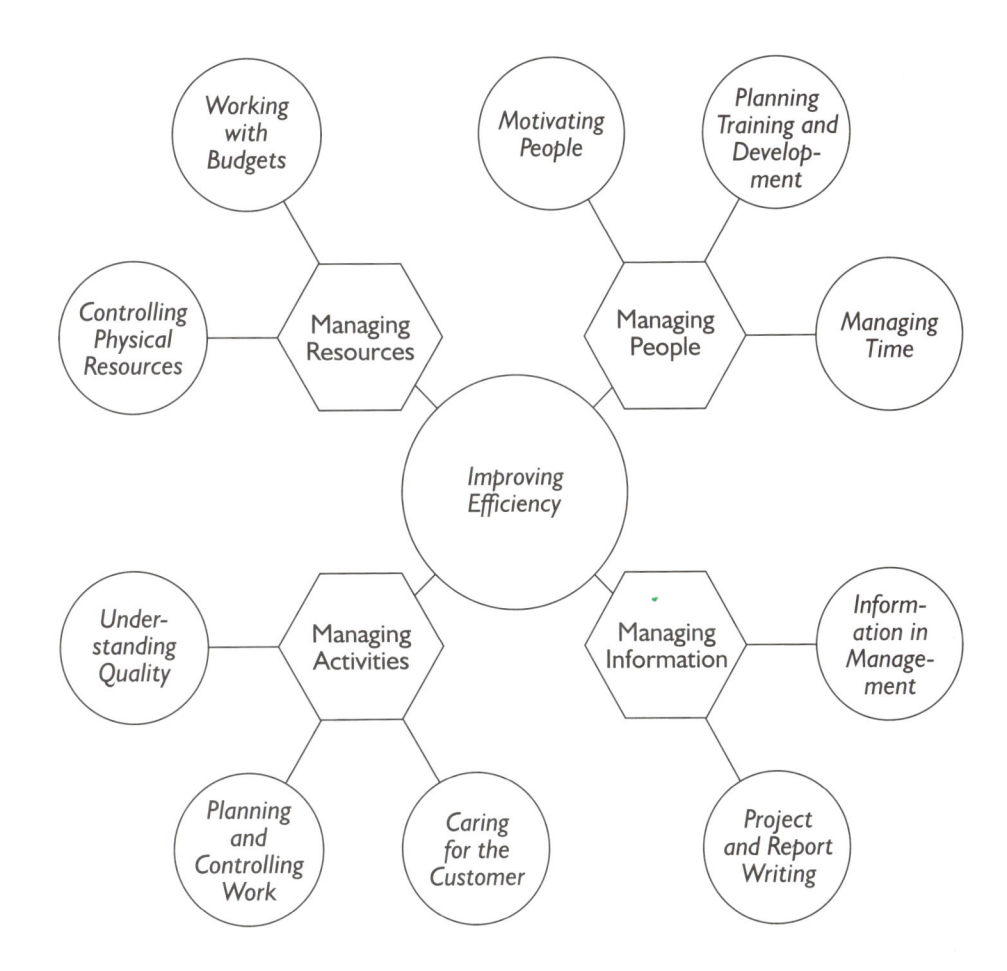

```
         Working                      Motivating      Planning
          with                         People         Training and
         Budgets                                      Development

Controlling          Managing              Managing           Managing
 Physical            Resources              People              Time
Resources

                         Improving
                         Efficiency

Under-               Managing               Managing         Information
standing             Activities            Information       in Manage-
Quality                                                         ment

         Planning                     Caring                   Project
          and                         for the                 and Report
       Controlling                   Customer                  Writing
          Work
```

v

Workbook introduction

2 S/NVQ links

This workbook relates to the following elements:

B1.1   Make recommendations for the use of resources
B1.2   Contribute to the control of resources

It will also help you to develop personal competence in communication and presentation, analysis, judgement and decision making, planning and prioritizing and commitment to excellence.

3 Workbook objectives

We talk continuously about the need to improve our productivity and, God knows, it is a dire need: yet we appear to accept with equanimity that in the world of work we are achieving less than half our capacity. Luckily for us few other countries do much better, but the potential for improvement is so vast that it is incomprehensible that we do not debate, study and struggle to do better.

John Harvey-Jones (1995), *All Together Now*, Mandarin.

If you agree with Sir John's words, you can congratulate yourself. By taking up this workbook you have made the decision to study and debate productivity and efficiency.

What can you expect to learn? There are three sessions; the first and third can be summarized very concisely, as follows:

> **Work is about converting resources to outputs. These resources are capital, materials, information, energy, equipment, time, finance and people. It is in the optimum management of resources that efficiency is achieved. The manager desiring improvements in efficiency must therefore identify the resources at his or her command, and find ways of getting the best from them.**

Although Session B is not central to this theme, it is very relevant, and you should find it informative. It deals with ways of measuring and analysing work processes: productivity, work study, and some of the latest thinking about how to improve the efficiency of organizations.

All organizations would like their employees to be more efficient, because **efficiency** is normally equated with profitability. One way of expressing efficiency is as an equation: what you get out, divided by what you put in. **Effectiveness**, on the other hand has to do with how good you are at achieving what you set out to achieve.

> A story which illustrates the distinction between efficiency and effectiveness is that of a surgeon who was said to have improved his efficiency by completing more operations in a day, only to reduce his effectiveness, as all his patients died.

Workbook introduction

One misplaced fear is that increased efficiency leads to job losses; the argument is that fewer people will be needed to perform the same tasks. In fact, the opposite is generally true. When efficiency goes up, an organization becomes more prosperous, is able to expand its sphere of activities, and so more people are likely to be needed.

3.1 Objectives

At the end of this workbook you will be *better able to*:

- recognize what efficiency means in the context of your workplace;
- identify and use some work study techniques to help you improve efficiency and effectiveness;
- plan for the best use of resources assigned to you;
- contribute effectively to the control of your organization's resources;
- play your part in helping to improve the efficiency of your workteam and your organization.

4 Activity planner

The following Activities require some planning so you may want to look at these now.

- Activity 28 on page 60 starts the process of creating a structured approach to increasing efficiency by finding ways to advance the potential of your team. This is continued in Activity 34 on page 67.
- Activity 29 on page 61 helps you to make optimum use of your workspace. You might like to start making a note of problems and requirements now. This is continued in Activity 35 on page 68.
- Activity 30 on page 62 provides the basis of a structured approach to better use of your equipment. This is continued in Activity 36 on page 69.
- Activity 31 on page 63 provides the basis of a structured approach to increased efficiency in the use of materials. This is continued in Activity 37 on page 70.
- Activity 33 on page 65 provides the basis of a structured approach to improving the use you make of sources of information. This is continued in Activity 39 on page 72.

Portfolio of evidence

Some or all of these Activities may provide the basis of evidence for your S/NVQ portfolio. All Portfolio Activities and the Work-based assignment are signposted with this icon.

The icon states the elements to which the Portfolio Activities and Work-based assignment relate.

Workbook introduction

The Work-based assignment (on page 78) asks you to develop one pair of these Activities into a complete plan for improving efficiency with respect to one resource at your command. This could also be used to form the basis for your portfolio of evidence, and should be useful in helping to demonstrate your Personal Competence in:

- obtaining the commitment of others;
- analysing and conceptualizing, by showing that you can think clearly and objectively about the past, and to apply your thinking to present and future plans;
- teambuilding skills;
- focusing on results;
- making decisions;
- and your commitment to excellence.

You may want to prepare for it in advance.

Session A Background to efficiency

1 Introduction

> Except for the rare monopoly situation, the only thing that differentiates one business from another in any given field is the quality of its management on all levels. And the only way to measure this crucial factor is through a measurement of productivity that shows how well resources are utilised and how much they yield.
>
> Peter F Drucker, *The Practice of Management.*[1]

Managers need to have many qualities, including: industry, honesty, self-confidence, a sense of fairness, moral courage, consistency, audacity. Commendable as these attributes are, they are very difficult to measure, and they don't **necessarily** lead to good results for the organization. Efficiency (or productivity), on the other hand, can usually be calculated, and the efficient manager is recognized as a successful manager.

Taking another view, the work managers do can be said to consist of:

- achieving desired results by giving direction to others;
- balancing efficiency and effectiveness;
- getting the most from limited resources.

The last two of these are the subjects of this workbook.

This session aims to help you get a good understanding of efficiency and effectiveness at work.

---

[1] Paperback edition (1989), page 68, Butterworth-Heinemann.

Session A

2 Work organizations

It can be useful to classify work organizations into four groups or sectors. We have the:

- **manufacturing sector**, where goods are produced;
- **transport sector**, in which people or goods are transferred;
- **supply sector**, which supplies goods it does not manufacture;
- **service sector**, where services, rather than physical goods, are passed to the customer.

Activity 1

2 mins

Which sector or sectors do your employers fall into?

Service Sector.

Most organizations are not difficult to categorize. All manufacturers, of whatever commodity, are obviously in the first group. Apart from industrial companies, manufacturing includes agriculture, the construction industry, and the energy producers, i.e. generators of electricity, and manufacturers of gas and oil products.

Airlines, bus companies and freight companies are all in the transportation business. Shops, distributors, car dealers and so on fall into the supply sector. The service sector includes such organizations as hairdressers, building societies, restaurants etc.

Of course, some companies, especially the larger corporations, can claim to be represented in more than one sector. Marks and Spencer plc, for example, supplies clothes and food, and offers financial services. The Virgin group's enterprises include shops (supply), radio broadcasting (service), and an airline (transport). Also, some industries really straddle two sectors: holiday travel companies are not simply in the business of transporting people; their main aim is to offer a service.

Which of these four sectors is the largest?

In many countries, including the UK, the service sector has long since supplanted manufacturing as the largest group, with that trend likely to continue.

You may read or hear people lamenting the 'decline of our great manufacturing industries'. In the United States, the same sentiments are often

> According to the Department for Education and Employment, the total number of people in employment in the UK in September 1995 was 21 911 000. In November, 3 853 000 were in manufacturing employment in Great Britain.

Session A

expressed. These complaints may be justified, in the sense that those countries with a strong manufacturing base have traditionally been among the richest. However, there are many who argue that this is less true today. Britain may make fewer cars and tractors than it used to, but it exports a vast range of services, which earn a great deal of money and prestige.

Whatever you think about this, you will perhaps agree that it is silly to suggest that one work sector is somehow more 'worthy' than another. Real work is done in all organizations!

But we are getting away from our subject. Let's now turn to the question of what work itself consists of.

3 Work as a transforming process

When we do work on something, we change it in some way. A wood-turner takes a piece of wood and (literally) turns it into a chair leg; a skilled gardener can transform a plot of rough ground into a delight to the eye by filling it with flowers and shrubs; a builder changes bricks and mortar into houses. Another way of putting it is to say that all work is a **transforming** process.

Thus we can say that work organizations of all kinds carry out transformations. In its simplest form, the work process is shown by the following diagram:

Inputs → Transformations → Outputs

Transformations consist of one or more of three types:

- **improving**
- **caretaking**
- **transferring**.

The simplest examples to identify are those in the manufacturing sector. A power station has inputs of water plus coal, oil or nuclear fuel, and it 'improves' these inputs first to steam and then to electricity, its final output. Textile mills transform fibres into cloth. To 'improve' is another way of saying 'add value to'.

The inputs and outputs of a school happen to be the same: children. The transformations taking place here are those of caretaking – safeguarding through a period of time, and improving – increasing the children's knowledge and understanding.

What about transferring? We can say that a taxi company 'transforms' people by transferring them to their desired destination, while taking care of them during the journey. A waste disposal company is also in the business of transferring and caretaking.

Session A

Activity 2

4 mins

Jot down the inputs, transformation processes and outputs of your own organization (or, if there are many, **three** or **four** of them).

Inputs	Transformation type	Outputs
Children with difficulties	Caretaking & improving	Reduction in difficulty.
Teachers managing difficulties	Caretaking/transforming	Better management of difficulties.
Excluded pupils	Caretaking/transforming	Placement for new start

In case you had difficulty with this, I'll give a few more examples.

An airline transfers people from one place to another (movement in space), while taking care of them through time, and (conceivably) 'improving' them by making them more rested, or better fed.

A chiropodist improves people by attending to their feet. Financial advisers have as their inputs the financial affairs of their clients, which they aim to improve by proposing sound investments. A baker converts flour and yeast into bread and cakes. Farmers take as inputs seeds, soil and fertilizers in order to produce outputs of crops. The inputs of beauticians could be said to be the faces and bodies of their customers, which they try to improve by making them more beautiful.

> **EXTENSION 1**
> *Operations Management*, John Naylor. Most of the topics covered in this workbook are typically included under the general topic area of **operations management**.

Operations management is defined in the book of the same name by John Naylor as follows:

Operations management is concerned with creating, operating and controlling a transformation system which takes inputs of a variety of resources and produces outputs of goods and services which are needed by customers.

4 Introduction to resources

The inputs to work processes are called **resources**, which can be classified in at least three ways. You may see resources separated into:

- <u>m</u>oney
- <u>m</u>anpower
- <u>m</u>achines and
- <u>m</u>aterials

– the four Ms.

Session A

A second classification is 'land, capital and labour'. Here, land is the term used to describe all natural resources, including water, airspace and raw materials. Capital is all non-human, non-natural resources, and labour is the term used for human resources.

However, the most usual way of categorizing resources, and the one we will use, is:

- people
- capital
- materials
- information.

Let's look at what we mean by these four groups.

- **People** (also called **labour**): those who run the organization, and work in it

    It should be said from the start that many object to applying the word 'resource' to people. For example, John Harvey-Jones, in his book *All Together Now*, says:

    I am by nature a mild-mannered man who likes to consider himself tolerant and understanding; however, when people are referred to as 'human resources' and are evaluated in the same way as money, raw materials or technology, a red haze settles over my eyes. People are not a resource, they are people – in their glory, variety and ability.

    You may agree with this view: it does seem strange and unfeeling to think of people as a resource. We do this simply for convenience. But it is important to remember, when bracketing employees alongside capital, materials and information, that:

    people are the most precious, most flexible and most necessary of all the resources of an organization.

    Without people to organize and direct the work, nothing worthwhile can be achieved, even in those workplaces where there is a high level of automation.

    Getting the best from people, whether or not you classify them as a resource, is the most challenging aspect of a manager's job.

- **Capital**: equipment, machinery, finance, land, and buildings

    We define capital as the permanent or semi-permanent assets of the organization, apart from people, which are needed to enable goods and services to be produced.

    Deciding how equipment, finance, land, and buildings can be used to best effect occupies much of the time and efforts of management.

Session A

- **Materials**: raw materials and components, which are converted or consumed by the process, together with the energy consumed

    These are the direct inputs: the ingredients which are used up in producing the goods or services that are the outputs of an organization.

    Frequently, this is the group of resources where the most waste occurs, and which consequently has the greatest potential for savings and improved efficiency.

- **Information**: a vital resource, which includes the know-how to do the work, knowledge of competitors and markets and so on

    No work can be done without intelligence. Often, it is the best informed managers who are the most effective and efficient.

Time is sometimes listed as a separate resource, and is certainly a constraining factor in all human endeavour.

It is difficult to think of an organization which can operate without every one of these resources. Our model can therefore be modified to:

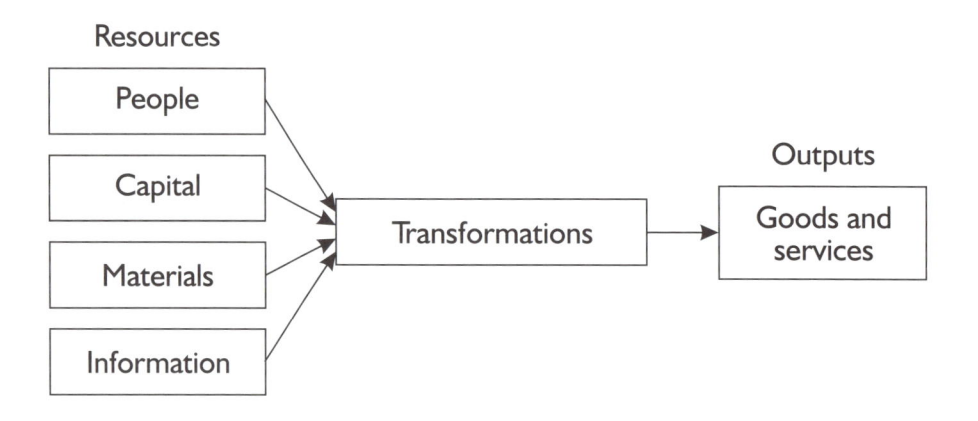

Resources: People, Capital, Materials, Information → Transformations → Outputs: Goods and services

Activity 3 (3 mins)

Now think about your own organization again, and list a few of its resources as people, capital, materials and information. Jot down just **three** examples of each type.

People: _Colleagues, managers, supporting organisation/admin_
Capital: _Office, buildings, infrastructure_
Materials: _Computer, car, paper/admin_
Information: _Procedures, materials, policies, communication, knowledge about clients._

Answers to this Activity can be found on page 87.

Session A

We need to go on to discuss resources in more detail, but before doing that, we should return to our main theme: efficiency and effectiveness.

5 Efficiency

By defining exactly what we mean by efficiency and effectiveness, we will have a better idea how resources can be used efficiently and effectively.

Activity 4 (2 mins)

How would you define the word 'efficiency'?

[Handwritten response:]
- A measure of transfer from input to output.
- The successness in effecting that transfer.
- Best use of resources to effect that transfer.

There are several ways to express what efficiency means; compare your answer with the following. Efficiency has been defined as:

- 'a measure of how well resources are transformed into outputs'
- 'working well with little waste'
- 'getting the most out from what you put in'
- 'the production of the maximum result from the minimum effort'
- 'the best use of resources, to achieve production of goods or services'.

The last definition is the one most meaningful in the context of this workbook. To be efficient, we must make the best use of resources, i.e., we have to find ways of utilizing resources to produce the goods or services we want, with the minimum of waste. To repeat the definition:

Efficiency means making the best use of resources, in achieving production of goods or services.

The main purpose of the workbook is to investigate ways in which this can be done. Relevant activities in achieving efficiency at work are likely to include:

- developing existing resources;
- reducing the amount or cost of resources;
- utilizing existing resources in the best way;
- finding better resources than the ones we have.

Session A

6 Why is efficiency important?

It may seem obvious to say that all organizations want to be more efficient. But why? What is the effect of increased efficiency? So far as any commercial company is concerned, the answer can be summed up in the following diagram:

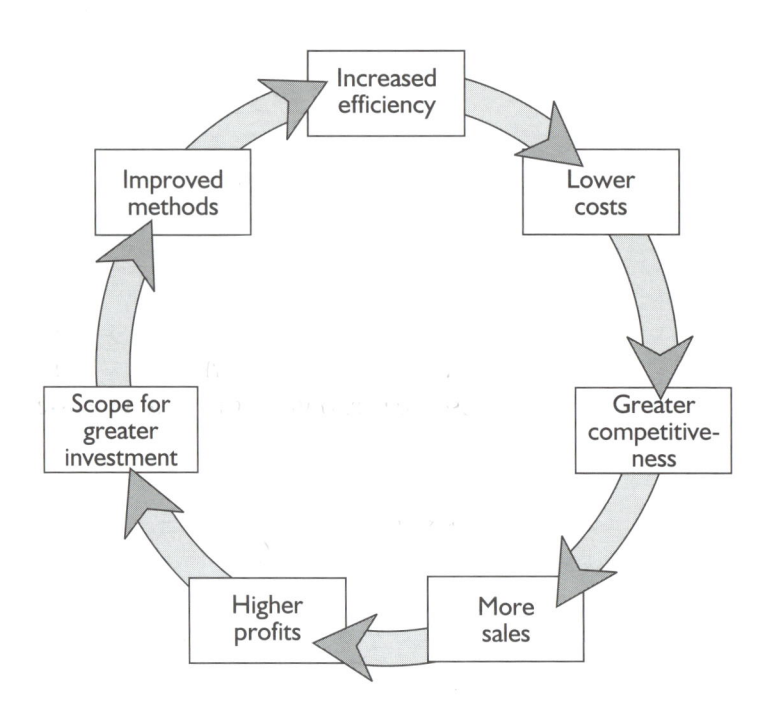

```
Increased efficiency → Lower costs → Greater competitiveness → More sales → Higher profits → Scope for greater investment → Improved methods → Increased efficiency
```

As you can see, the effects are self-regenerating. As efficiency increases, so costs go down, and the organization has leeway to reduce prices, resulting in enhanced competitiveness. This leads to higher sales and profits, and opens the way for the organization to invest in even better methods of production. Efficiency can then be raised even more, and the cycle continues.

Activity 5 *(2 mins)*

What will be the effect of reduced efficiency? Explain briefly how the above diagram would be altered if this were the case.

Higher costs, lower sales + therefore lower profits. Methods tending to be wasteful. Lower potential for investment.

Answers to this Activity can be found on page 87.

8

Session A

7 Effectiveness

Peter Drucker, a well-known management guru, described efficiency as 'doing things right', and effectiveness as 'doing the right things'.

Effectiveness has also been defined as:

- 'an assessment of how far a stated objective is achieved'
- 'being concerned with the achievement of set organizational goals or objectives'.

There is an important distinction between efficiency and effectiveness. It is perfectly possible to be efficient and yet ineffective, as you read in the Workbook introduction. The jeweller who saves on materials while producing brooches that no one wants to wear can hardly claim to have attained her objectives. Effectiveness without efficiency is also conceivable, but less likely; people at work who achieve objectives while being wasteful of resources should not expect applause.

7.1 Objectives

Activity 6 (4 mins)

Summarize, briefly, the stated objectives of your workteam.

To work as efficiently and effectively as possible to support pupils, their families and schools in matching difficulties.

It isn't possible to know how you answered, but they would be an unusual set of objectives if they did not include reference to your customers – the people you provide goods or services to. Workteam objectives are typically expanded versions of the following:

> 'We aim to provide a first class service (or high quality goods) to our customers, in an efficient manner.'

Your customers may be another team, or they may be the customers of the organization itself.

Session A

All commercial enterprises must ultimately direct their activities towards satisfying their customers. Even non-commercial organizations, such as charities and schools, can be said to have customers. So our earlier model of work organizations should be modified just once more to give:

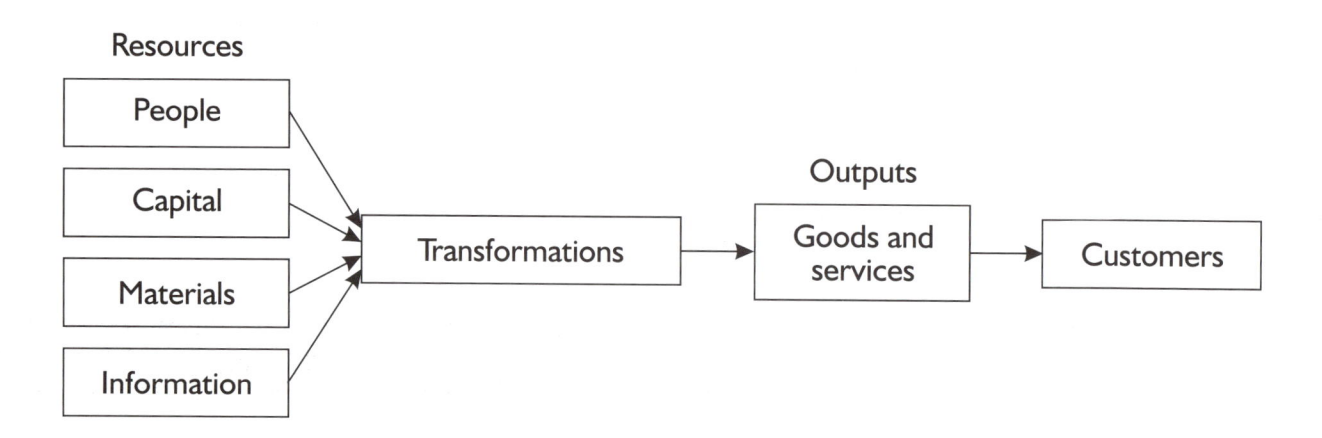

```
Resources: People, Capital, Materials, Information → Transformations → Outputs: Goods and services → Customers
```

Work organizations transform resources (capital, materials and information, with the help of people) into goods and services, which are provided to their customers.

This model can help us identify sources of inefficiency and ineffectiveness.

Activity 7

3 mins

Jot down **two** ways in which you could be more **inefficient** in your job.

Making no note of action points.
Making no effort to be on time or attend meetings.

Now note **two** ways in which you might become more **ineffective**.

Prioritise only those things I like doing.
Ignore what people say and do my own thing.

Answers to this Activity can be found on page 87.

A manicurist could be inefficient by wasting materials, turning up late for appointments and so on. Ineffectiveness might presumably be accomplished by breaking the clients' nails.

If a school canteen were to spoil food, it would be less than fully efficient. But if it were to cook insufficient meals for the number of children to be served, so that some went hungry, it would be less than fully effective.

Session A

In a similar way, a bricklayer who damaged new bricks might be called inefficient. Building a crooked wall, though, should cause the bricklayer to be labelled both ineffective (in not achieving the aim of building a straight wall), *and* inefficient (in thereby causing the wall to have to be built again).

If we want to be efficient and effective, we have to find ways of doing the opposite kinds of things from those mentioned above.

The concept of effectiveness is relevant to all jobs, and efficiency is relevant to nearly all, no matter what products or services are provided by the organization.

8 Quality

There's one other very relevant topic worth taking a look at before getting back to the subject of resources, and that is 'quality'.

Activity 8

4 mins

How would you define 'high quality'? Try to sum up the meaning of these words in a couple of sentences. You could start by thinking about what you mean by high quality as a customer, when you buy something in a shop, say.

Conforming to a high standard of product or service. A measure of excellence ~ the best there is giving good value for money.

You might say that high quality means:

- getting the kind of products and services that you want;
- conforming to a high standard; or
- the best there is;
- excellence.

These are all correct, so far as they go.

When we want to buy something – whether it is food, clothing, luxury items or any other product – we usually have a good deal of choice. There may be a number of different shops and outlets selling goods made by a number of different manufacturers.

11

Session A

Because of all this choice, the goods and services which best meet the needs of customers will sell well. The goods and services which fail to provide customers with what they want will not sell so well – or may not sell at all.

Quality is in fact concerned with **every** aspect of a product.

Quality can be defined as all the features and characteristics of a product or service which affect its ability to satisfy the needs of customers and users.

This definition provides a clue to the link between efficiency, effectiveness and quality. We have already agreed that effectiveness means the achievement of objectives, and that the objectives of all commercial organizations are inevitably linked to satisfying customers.

It is the most effective organizations who are best able to achieve high standards of quality, by delivering the products and services that their customers want. And it is the most efficient ones who are able to survive and prosper in competitive markets.

We will not dwell further upon the subject of quality in this workbook. Other Super Series 3 units deal with it in some depth.

However, before we move on, it is worth mentioning 'the **five rights of customers**'. These are the aspects of quality that every customer has a right to expect; they are:

- the right product or service
- of the right quality
- at the right time
- in the right place
- at the right price.

Only when a commercial organization consistently delivers products or services which meet these expectations, can it say it is being fully effective in its objectives in satisfying its customers.

In the next three sections, we return to the subject of resources.

9 People as a resource

On page 5 we listed the resources which are inputs to the work process. They are:

- people
- capital
- materials
- information.

Let's look at people first.

Session A

Activity 9

12 mins

Read the following statements carefully, and comment upon them. In each case, tick the appropriate box to indicate whether you think it is, in your experience, 'accurate', 'partially accurate' or 'inaccurate'. Then write a sentence or two explaining the reason for your choice. Think about your own organization as you answer.

	Accurate	Partially accurate	Inaccurate

I think the employees of an organization are typically:

a an underdeveloped resource;   [ ] [✓] [ ]

  because _initiatives are taken but nothing gets properly finished._

b more caring about, and interested in, their work than most employers recognize;   [✓] [ ] [ ]

  because _employers priorities do not always coincide with what is understood about the needs at the 'sharp end'._

c an undervalued resource;   [ ] [✓] [ ]

  because _success is not always reflected back in a 'hearts and minds' way._

d treated as if they could easily be replaced;   [ ] [✓] [ ]

  because _their well being is not considered in the management of change._

e less efficient or reliable than machines;   [ ] [✓] [ ]

  because _alot depends upon how far an employer feels valued._

f the most adaptable, precious and potentially useful resource the organization has.   [✓] [ ] [ ]

  because _without them who would do the work!_

Your views on these statements are as valid as the next person's: there are no right or wrong answers. Compare your response with the following points.

a   There seems to be little doubt that, in many organizations, people are an underdeveloped resource. You may feel that you, or other members of your team, are not being given the opportunities to use your abilities to the full. Most employers create and define jobs, and then try to find the people to fill them. This is inevitably a difficult matching process. While many employees find themselves capable of fulfilling their assigned roles, they may in truth not feel well suited to the job they are made to do.

Session A

In smaller organizations, and in some enlightened larger ones, the task may be moulded to the individual, rather than the other way round. The question changes from one of 'What should the person in this job be doing?' to 'What are we as individuals capable of, and how can our combined skills be used to achieve our objectives?' This approach gives people greater scope for self-expression and development.

The subject of getting the best from people is taken up again in Session C.

b   A related question is that of whether employees are more caring about, and interested in, their work than most employers recognize. Again, your response will reflect your experience and point of view: it depends on the people, and on the employer. Most people do care about their jobs, and would be willing to contribute more, given some encouragement.

c,d   Are employees an undervalued resource? This is perhaps a more debatable point. If you decided this statement is accurate, it may be that you feel undervalued yourself, or have seen organizations or executives who treat their workers with scant regard.

Certainly, when so many people have lost their jobs in recent years (said to be over 5 million employees in the 1990s in the UK alone), an unbiased observer might think that employees are often treated as if they were expendable. 'Cost cutting' and 'improvements in efficiency' can sometimes seem to be an excuse for organizations to lay off staff.

e   Are people less efficient or less reliable than machines? Perhaps you will agree that there is some truth in this. When it comes to performing routine tasks repetitively, there is no contest: automated processes win easily. But the time has not yet come when machines can truly 'think'. We have not yet seen a factory where the intelligence and thinking efficiency of people is not needed. (However, who can say this will never happen?)

People at work do get 'replaced by machines', and the justification is usually an economic one. However, you don't *necessarily* increase efficiency simply by introducing more equipment: every case has to be considered on its merits.

f   You will perhaps agree that this last statement is accurate: employees are the most adaptable, precious and potentially useful resource the organization has.

As we will discuss later in the workbook, an important approach to achieving improvements in efficiency is in finding ways of getting the best from your team.

Session A

10 Capital as a resource

10.1 Land and buildings

The land and buildings of an organization, assuming they are owned outright, are usually among its most valuable assets. It goes without saying, therefore, that they should be used efficiently and effectively.

Activity 10 · 3 mins

What do you think is entailed in making effective and efficient use of land and buildings? Try to list **two** things.

Best use is made of the space for the work to be done – the space is adequate for the facilities.

Some points you may have mentioned are that buildings and land should be:

- maintained properly, so that they retain their value;
- allocated between people, sections and departments so that each group has the right amount of space and facilities, in the right location;
- developed to their full potential; for example, an old building may need to be demolished and replaced (subject to current planning regulations!), if it no longer serves the needs of the organization adequately.

10.2 Finance

By finance, we mean funds (i.e. available money) or the provision of funds. Of course, buildings, land and other resources are valuable, but they would first have to be sold before they could be used to purchase other things.

Unless you work in the finance department of your organization, the primary way in which you help to control finance will probably be through **budgets**.

> Budgets are itemized summaries of expected income and expenditure over a period.

Session A

In Session C, we will briefly discuss ways in which first line managers can contribute to the efficient use of finance. In the meantime, you might like to start giving some thought to the following questions. You may not feel you can write down answers straight away; if you can't, keep the questions in mind as you go about your work in the next few days.

Activity 11

5 mins

How could you keep the finance you are responsible for under better control?

By having more frequent reviews of cash flows and statements of accounts.

What further information, if any, would help you do this?

Seeing financial transactions through from ordering to authorising payment and sending it myself.

10.3 Equipment

Equipment and machinery are the tools of work, and may include items as diverse as screwdrivers, computers, knitting needles, ovens, sewing machines and welding gear. Often, machinery is both expensive and complicated, and requires a good deal of understanding if it is to be used efficiently. As with other assets, a proper schedule of maintenance is usually necessary.

Session A

10.4 Goodwill

The capital of an organization includes intangible items that are sometimes difficult to put a value on. Probably the most important of these is **goodwill**.

Activity 12 · 3 mins

Explain briefly what you understand by the term 'goodwill'.

The credibility integrity of the service as viewed by customers and clients.

How might goodwill be lost, and what will be the effects if it is lost?

Poor quality service, lack of response, perceptions of rudeness and giving a general impression of appearing to be uncaring.

As you might have said, the goodwill of an organization is the value of how it is seen by others. Goodwill has real worth, which can be realized when the organization is sold.

Goodwill may be lost by, for example:

- delivering poor quality goods or services to customers;
- dealing with customers in an high-handed fashion;
- failing to address complaints or concerns expressed by members of the public;
- having poor relations with the press;
- having an uncaring attitude to the environment.

In the case of commercial companies, the effects of lost goodwill are, sooner or later, loss of profits resulting from lost sales.

Loss of goodwill comes about through ineffectiveness or inefficiency, and leads to reduced profits.

Session A

11 Materials as a resource

Material resources are those things consumed (energy and consumable items) or converted (raw materials and components) during the work process.

Activity 13 — 2 mins

What items are consumed in your work area? Note down **two**, if you can.

Paper for writing, photocopying, printing etc. Fuel in order to meet appointments and carry out work

Hospitals consume hypodermic needles, drugs, bandages, and blood in converting sick people to well ones; printers consume ink in converting blank paper to printed copy; poachers consume shot-gun pellets in converting live animals to dead ones; laundries consume washing powder and water in converting dirty washing to clean.

If you can save on materials you will automatically become more efficient.

We'll return to this subject in Session C.

11.1 Energy

In all work processes, energy is used, even if it is only the energy consumed by human muscle.

In the modern world, electricity is of course the energy source which is in most common use. Without electricity, it seems that civilization would grind to a halt.

Like any other resource, fuels (electricity, gas, oil, petrol etc.) have to be paid for. Most organizations make some attempt to buy their energy supplies from the least expensive sources, and to reduce wasteful use. However, there are usually ways to improve efficiency through the careful management of energy. Every manager can contribute to these savings.

Session A

12 Time as a resource

Time is not always regarded as a separate resource because it is assumed to be part of the use of people. I think it is so important, however, that it is worth separate consideration here.

Sometimes, saving time can lead directly to increased efficiency. The rule is simple, and fairly obvious: if you can perform a task more quickly **without increasing your use of other resources**, then you have improved efficiency. If this is not the case, then the saving in time must be balanced against any extra costs involved. The following example illustrates this point.

■ Ron Wheeling was workshop supervisor at a garage. His job was to ensure that every customer's car was serviced to the owner's satisfaction. Over a period of time, Ron noticed that the average 'turn-round time' – the time from a car being left by a customer to when it was collected – had become longer. This was because more cars were being held over to a second or third day. Some customers had complained about this.

In his weekly meeting with Jim Pardhu, the garage owner, Ron produced figures showing that business had increased. He said he believed that they needed more staff to cope with the rise, and an extra servicing bay. 'If we don't get through more cars in a day,' Ron said, 'we will get more and more complaints.'

Jim wasn't convinced. 'If business is increasing, we must be doing something right – people must like us. I could take on more staff to cut down the average turn-round time, but that will reduce my profits, and I might not be able to give you and the team a rise at Christmas. I have to be sure that business will go on increasing before I put in more investment.'

Finding the right balance between resources like this is never easy. Often, there is not enough information to make a decision based entirely on the facts, especially where the behaviour of customers are concerned. In this case, the main question is whether increasing labour and capital resources in order to reduce another resource – time, would be justified in terms of higher income and profits.

Session A

Self-assessment 1

10 mins

1 Complete the following diagram, by writing in the correct words:

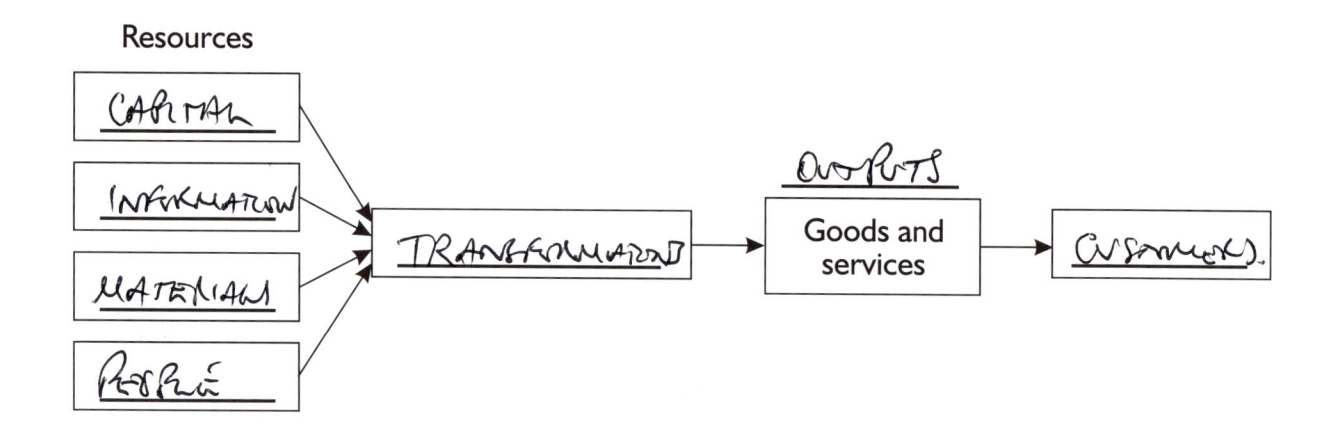

Resources

- CAPITAL
- INFORMATION
- MATERIALS
- PEOPLE

→ TRANSFORMATION → **OUTPUTS** Goods and services → CUSTOMERS

2 Place the following types of work organization in the most appropriate cells in the table:

a A UK regional electricity company.
b A UK water company.
c A hairdresser.
d A hardware shop.
e A residential school.
f A farm.

Transformation type	Sector			
	Manufacturing	Transport	Supply	Service
Improving	F			C E
Caretaking	F			E
Transferring	F	A	A B D	A B

20

Session A

3 Complete the following statements, by replacing the blanks with suitable words:

a _EFFICIENCY_ means making the best use of _RESOURCES_, to achieve production of goods or _SERVICES_.

b Work organizations _TURN_ resources (capital, materials and _INFORMATION_, with the help of _PEOPLE_) into goods and services, which are provided to their _CUSTOMERS/CLIENTS_

c _QUALITY_ can be defined as all the _FEATURES_ and characteristics of a product or service that affect its ability to _MEET_ the needs of customers and _USERS_.

d Loss of _GOODWILL_ comes about through _INEFFECTIVENESS_ or inefficiency, and leads to reduced _RETURNS/PROFITS_

Answers to these questions can be found on pages 84–5.

Session A

13 Summary

- Work organizations can be categorized into four sectors: manufacturing; transport; supply; service.
- Work can be described as a transforming process; transformations may consist of improving, caretaking or transferring.
- Resources are the inputs to the work process, and may be listed as people, capital, materials and information.
- Efficiency means making the best use of resources, to achieve production of goods or services.
- Effectiveness is concerned with the achievement of organizational goals or objectives.
- It is the most effective organizations who are best able to achieve high standards of quality, by delivering the products and services that their customers want. And it is the most efficient ones who are able to survive and prosper in competitive markets.
- People are the most adaptable, precious and potentially useful resource an organization has.
- The land and buildings of an organization, assuming they are owned outright, are usually among its most valuable assets, and therefore should be used efficiently and effectively.
- By finance, we mean funds (i.e. available money) or the provision of funds.
- Often, equipment is both expensive and complicated, and requires a good deal of understanding.
- The goodwill of an organization can be described as the value of how it is seen by others. It is lost through inefficiency or ineffectiveness.
- If you can save on materials, you will automatically become more efficient.
- Every manager can contribute to energy savings.
- If you can perform a task quicker without increasing your use of other resources, then you will have improved efficiency.

Session B Productivity and work study

1 Introduction

We know what efficiency is, but how can we measure it? How should we recognize it when we see it?

If possible, it would be useful to express efficiency in numerical terms, so that we have a sound basis for comparison. And if we were able to divide work activities into small elements, we could set a standard time for performing each one, and calculate how long a task 'should' take, compared with what it does take.

The techniques described in this session attempt to do these things. Productivity reduces efficiency to a simple ratio. Method study is the breaking down of tasks into individual elements, and then analysing them. Work measurement uses techniques to determine how long a qualified worker takes to do a specified job to a defined level of performance.

At the end of the session, we look at two newer approaches to improving processes (benchmarking and continuous improvement), and then look at measuring the performance of white collar workers.

2 Productivity

If you recall, our definition of efficiency was as follows.

Efficiency means making the best use of resources, to achieve production of goods or services.

In its simplest form, efficiency can be expressed as a ratio of what we get out for what we put in, i.e.:

$$\frac{output}{input}$$

This is **productivity**, and can be applied at a national as well as at organizational level.

Session B

Let's put some numbers into this ratio. Say the inputs – the resources used – for a certain job cost £1000 and the output was valued at £2000.

Then the input:output ratio would be

$$\frac{2000}{1000}$$

We can simplify this to

$$\frac{2}{1}$$

This is known as the job's productivity ratio.

If we wanted to get an increase in productivity we could either **increase** the output for the same input or **decrease** the input for the same output. If for example we could increase the output value from £2000 to £3000, the ratio would become

$$\frac{3}{1}$$

On the other hand, if the resource costs fell from £1000 to £500 (with the output still valued at £2000), the ratio would become

$$\frac{2}{0.5} \text{ or } \frac{4}{1}$$

In other words:

Productivity rises if the output is increased without increasing the input, or if the output stays the same but the input is decreased.

2.1 Company productivity ratios

Some examples of productivity ratios used in organizations are:

a $\quad \dfrac{\text{Sales}}{\text{Labour hours}}$

b $\quad \dfrac{\text{Sales}}{\text{Pay}}$

c $\quad \dfrac{\text{Value of shipments}}{\text{Labour and materials}}$

d $\quad \dfrac{\text{Value of production}}{\text{Cost of labour + materials + capital + overheads}}$

Session B

Activity 14

Consider the following example.

Suppose you own a vineyard, and have the aim of getting rich by making lots of high quality wine. You could measure your productivity as:

1. $$\frac{\text{Number of bottles of wine produced}}{\text{Number of hectares of vineyard}}$$

2. $$\frac{\text{Value of wine produced}}{\text{Labour costs}}$$

3. $$\frac{\text{Value of wine produced}}{\text{Cost of all resources used}}$$

a Which ratio would give you the best overall indication of efficiency? Tick your answer.

1 ☐ 2 ☐ 3 ☑

b Are all these ratios true measures of efficiency? Encircle your answer.

Yes / **No**

Explain your answer to question (b):

In 2 the lower you work does not necessarily improve the value of the wine - equally low labour costs wouldn't improve the value of the wine if it was harvested at the wrong time.

Perhaps you will agree that ratio 3 is the best overall indication of efficiency. But what about the answer to (b)?

Suppose now that in one year in your vineyard you have a good crop of grapes, but make a mistake and pick them at the wrong time. You would probably still be able to make large quantities of wine, but it wouldn't be very good. You might have to sell the wine at a price that barely made you a profit.

If you used ratio 1, you could claim that your productivity was high, in terms of yield per hectare. This is a perfectly valid measure of productivity, and is the kind of figure used to compare the output of one vineyard with another. However, if you picked your crop at the wrong time you can hardly profess to have made 'the best use of resources', so your efficiency cannot be said to be high. (Incidentally, your effectiveness would not be very good, either, as you will have failed in your aims.)

Session B

Often, ratios and other statistical information can be misleading, and it is important to think carefully about what the figures really mean. In the above case, the key difference was that ratio 1 was in terms of the number of bottles, not the wine's value. In commercial organizations, it is sensible to assess overall productivity as a ratio of money: cost and value.

3 Work study

3.1 Introduction to work study

Earlier, you read about ways of expressing and measuring productivity. We've established that you increase productivity by becoming more efficient. But how do you become more efficient?

Often, though not always, this involves examining work methods. Doing this might lead you to change the way the workplace is laid out, change the sequence in which things are done, change an administrative system so you can make better use of computer power and so on. The systematic examination of work methods is called **work study**, which is what we are going to look at now.

The following sections will only provide a brief introduction to this rather specialized subject; they will:

- give you a taster of what work study tools and techniques are available and some suggestions for how you might pursue your studies further if you want to;
- provide you with some insight into the methods used by a specialist department or by outside consultants. If you work in a large organization you may occasionally become involved in a work study exercise carried out by experts. You will need to understand what they are doing and want to contribute effectively to the exercise. For one thing, it will be important for you to make sure they have got the right information about what happens in your work area.
- enable you to apply some of the techniques described. Although this brief introduction won't make you a work study expert, you might be able to explore a problem of, for example, traffic through your work area, or to record, in a systematic way, the operations carried out by one of your team.

Session B

3.2 What is work study?

> **EXTENSIONS 1 AND 2**
> The books listed in these extensions (on page 83) will enable you to find out more about work study.

In most kinds of jobs, efficiency depends (at least partly) on the methods used to do the work. **Work study** aims to analyse work methods, and the materials and equipment used, in order to:

determine the most economical way of doing the work;
standardize the method, and install it as standard practice;
establish the time required by a qualified and trained worker to carry out the job, at a defined level of performance.

Work study has two distinct but related aspects: **method study** and **work measurement**. The following diagram gives definitions of method study and work measurement, and shows how they are used together to improve productivity and efficiency.

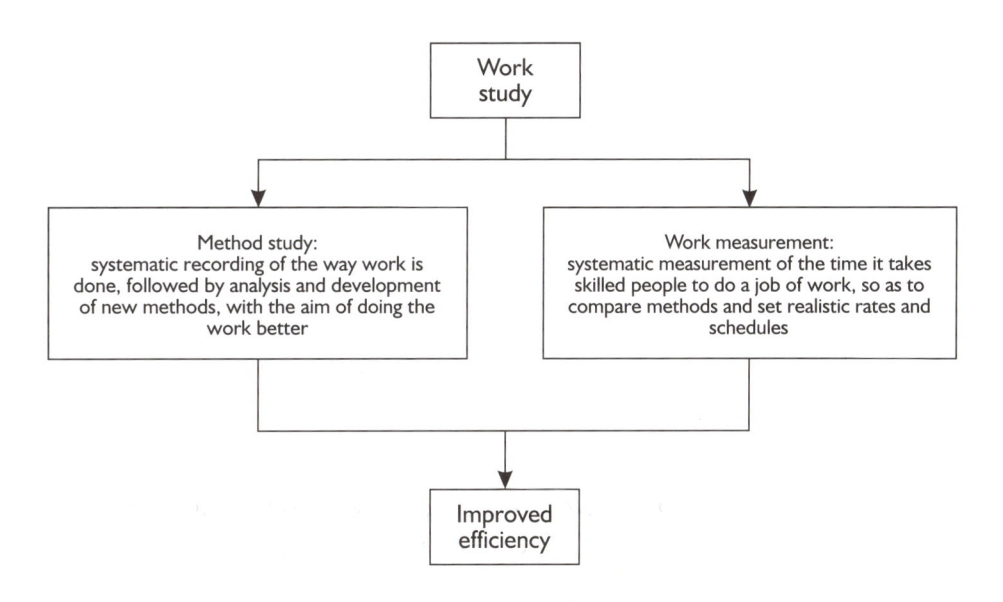

```
                    Work
                    study
                   /      \
                  ↓        ↓
    Method study:           Work measurement:
    systematic recording    systematic measurement
    of the way work is      of the time it takes
    done, followed by       skilled people to do a
    analysis and            job of work, so as to
    development of new      compare methods and set
    methods, with the aim   realistic rates and
    of doing the work       schedules
    better
                  \        /
                   ↓      ↓
                   Improved
                   efficiency
```

4 Method study

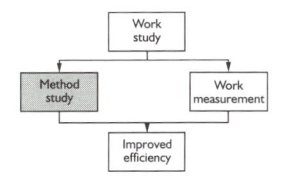

Essentially, method study involves breaking a job down into individual elements, and then analysing them. By probing and questioning, we hope to eliminate ineffective and inefficient methods and procedures and replace them with better ones.

There are six steps to method study. These steps may overlap, but it is important that they are all carried out, and in the following sequence:

1 **Select** the problem or work area to be studied.

2 **Record** what is actually taking place at the moment.

Session B

3 **Examine** and analyse what has been recorded and find out any inefficiencies or shortcomings in existing methods.

4 **Develop** alternatives to existing methods which are both new and improved.

5 **Define** and **install** the new method(s).

6 **Maintain** the newly installed method(s), to make sure they have achieved the required level of efficiency.

The following diagram shows these six steps:

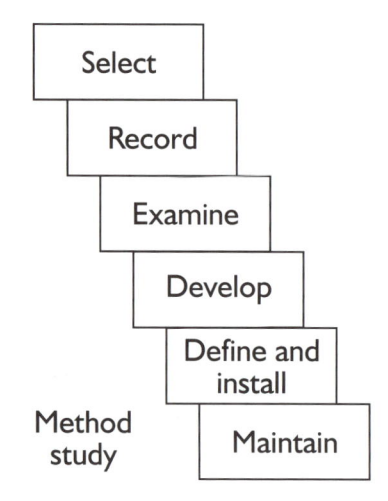

```
                    Select
                      Record
                        Examine
                          Develop
                            Define and
                              install
    Method                     Maintain
    study
```

These steps can be remembered by the initial letters of the words: SREDDIM (**S**heep **r**arely **e**at **d**ead **d**aisies **i**n **M**ay).

By following these steps, you can be sure of adopting a sound approach to method study techniques, whether you are tackling a large or a small job. The steps should help you:

- focus on the problem you're trying to solve;
- write down your findings, so you can consider them more easily;
- not to jump to conclusions;
- decide what action you're going to take;
- make sure your new method works, and keeps on working.

Session B

5 Selection

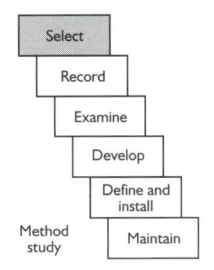

Selection is the process of choosing, by systematic means, a specific problem to be solved or an area of work to be studied, taking into account:

- the potential savings;
- the costs of an investigation;
- the anticipated life of the project.

Some examples of problems are:

- a production process which is found to have unacceptably high scrap costs;
- a particular work area being badly laid out, resulting in people or processes getting in the way of one another;
- inconsistent quality in a product or service – sometimes good, sometimes not so good;
- excessive overtime being worked;
- a lot of complaints by customers, or by employees.

Activity 15

3 mins

Suppose you recognize a problem in your work area which you feel ought to be investigated if possible. You suggest to your boss that method study could usefully be applied to this problem.

What considerations might influence your organization in its decision whether or not to begin a method study project? For instance, one consideration would be 'How much money could we expect to save by carrying out this work?'

Try to write down **three** other questions that might be asked.

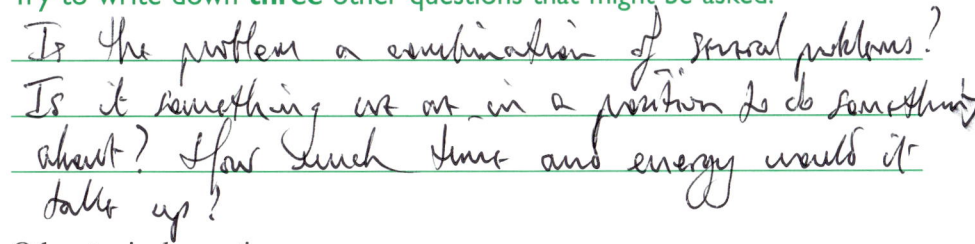

Is the problem a combination of several problems? Is it something we are in a position to do something about? How much time and energy would it take up?

Other typical questions are:

- Is the problem one which we will be able to do anything about?
- Do we have the time to do this work?
- Do we have the people and other resources available?
- Is it technically feasible to overcome the problem?
- How much disruption would the work cause?

You may have thought of several other questions.

Session B

There are three main considerations in selecting a problem for method study:

- **Financial** considerations – the impact on the organization's finances

   Specifically. when looking at projects from the financial point of view, we need to take into account:

   - the potential savings;
   - the costs of the investigation;
   - the anticipated life of the project.

- **Technical** considerations – the effects of techniques and technology

   Solving problems at work often means using technical solutions. At other times the technology itself forces changes to be made, as for instance when out-of-date equipment must be replaced.

- **human** considerations – the effects on the people

   Investigation into a problem or work area in order to improve productivity implies change. People often react against change. Sometimes they feel threatened by it: they may fear loss of job or of status or of income, for example. That's one reason why no investigation should be undertaken lightly.

   And when changes are planned, management will have to 'sell' the idea of the proposed new procedures and systems to the employees affected by them.

   These days, there may well be a fourth consideration: the possible impact on the local **environment** may have to be thought through, before starting the project.

6 Recording using process charts

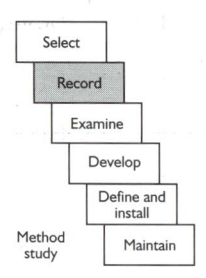

Systematic recording involves following a plan and using some special techniques. Work study officers (also known as management services officers or consultants) use a range of recording techniques which enable them to:

- record all the relevant facts in a standardized way;
- form as clear a picture as possible of what is going on.

Five activities have been identified, which can be used to describe work activities of many kinds; each has been assigned a special symbol.

Session B

6.1 Chart symbols

○	**Operation:**	(Remember 'O' for operation.)
□	**Inspection:**	(Think of looking at something through a square window.)
⇨	**Transport:**	(The arrow suggests movement.)
D	**Delay:**	(Looks like a 'D' for delay.)
▽	**Storage:**	(Imagine a cone-shaped storage container.)

There are variations on these symbols, but the ones above are the most commonly used and understood.

We will now use these symbols to create a chart which records a whole work process.

Let us follow the steps taken by Chandra, personal assistant to Personnel Manager Jenny Becconsall, typing a letter on a word-processor. Jenny has recorded a letter on a dictation machine, so Chandra starts by picking up the tape.

1	Chandra goes into Jenny's office to collect the tape casette	⇨	Transport
2	Chandra collects the tape	○	Operation
3	She returns to her own office	⇦	Transport
4	She then places the tape cassette onto her transcribing machine	○	Operation
5	Next, Chandra sets up the word-processing program	○	Operation
6	She then types the letter	○	Operation
7	She checks the letter for mistakes	□	Inspection
8	Chandra then prints the letter …	○	Operation
9	… and places it in a folder	○	Operation
10	She carries the folder into Jenny's office	⇨	Transport
11	Chandra has nothing to do while Jenny reads and signs the letter	D	Delay
12	Finally, she carries the signed letter back to her own office	⇦	Transport

Notice that to show a return journey the **transport** symbol is drawn in the opposite direction.

31

Session B

By recording the activities of a job using these symbols, the whole job can be set down and summarized on what is called a **flow process chart**. The flow process chart for Chandra's part of the process is shown below:

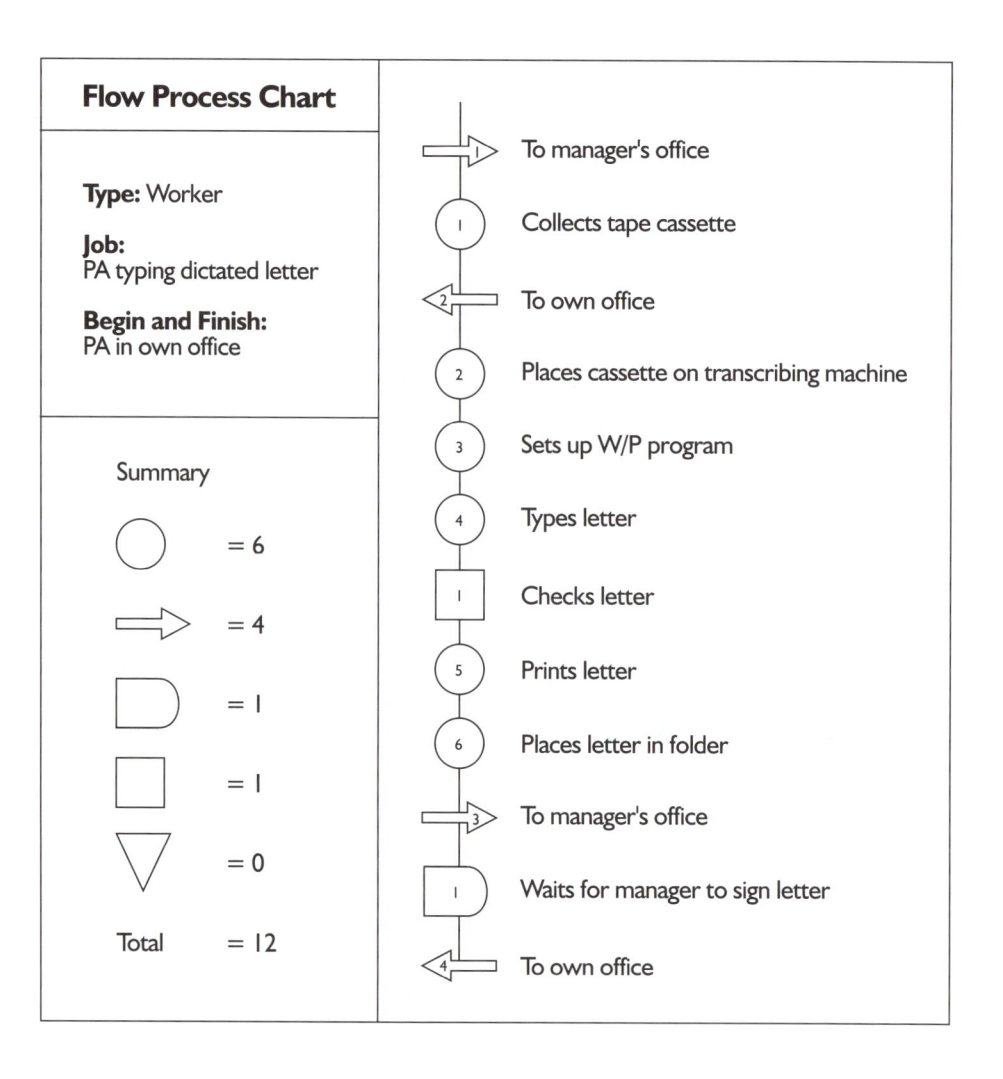

Flow Process Chart

Type: Worker

Job: PA typing dictated letter

Begin and Finish: PA in own office

Summary

○ = 6
⇨ = 4
⌓ = 1
☐ = 1
▽ = 0

Total = 12

- ⇨1 To manager's office
- ○1 Collects tape cassette
- ⇨2 To own office
- ○2 Places cassette on transcribing machine
- ○3 Sets up W/P program
- ○4 Types letter
- ☐1 Checks letter
- ○5 Prints letter
- ○6 Places letter in folder
- ⇨3 To manager's office
- ⌓1 Waits for manager to sign letter
- ⇨4 To own office

If you look at this chart carefully, you can see that

- symbols of a particular type are numbered sequentially;
- there is a summary of the number of times each type of symbol is used.

A flow process chart may be concerned with either materials, workers, equipment, information, or any combination of these. The above chart showed the activities from the point of view of the secretary. The chart could be redrawn, recording the activities from the point of view of the contents of the letter (or of the typewriter or dictating machine, perhaps).

A flow process chart can be used to record activities involving people, information, materials or equipment.

Session B

There is obviously more to preparing flow process charts than we have described here. You are not now expected to be able to draw up these charts: it takes training and practice, and is usually carried out by specialists. However, from this basic understanding of the procedure, you are in a good position to:

- investigate the subject further, should you need to;
- understand a flow process chart, if one is presented to you.

7 Other recording techniques

Process charts are a very valuable aid in recording the activities of a work process. However, they can't tell the complete story.

Activity 16

3 mins

Can you think of one or two other kinds of fact you might want to record about a work process, apart from the activities we've already discussed?

Time taken to complete task.
Distances involved in transport/transit
Amount of work carried in transit.

Other examples of information you might wish to record are:

- paths of movement: the actual route of travel within the work area;
- the distance: how many metres travelled;
- the time taken: how many minutes or hours for each activity.

Let's look first at a diagram which helps to show paths of movement.

Session B

7.1 Flow process diagrams

The same symbols as in flow process charts are used, except that they are drawn onto a scale diagram of the work area.

Here is an extract from a flow process chart showing two sets of activities involved in the manufacture of timber moulds. Note that the two are drawn side by side, which means they are likely to take place at the same time.

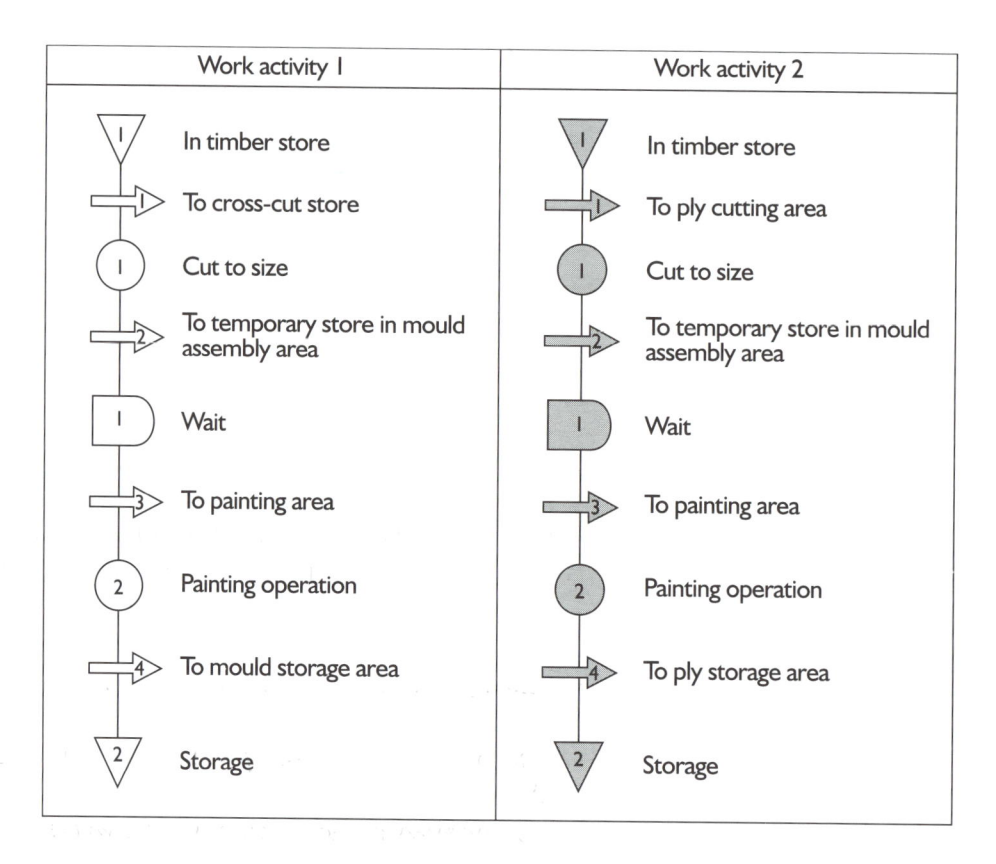

Work activity 1	Work activity 2
▽1 In timber store	▽1 In timber store
▷1 To cross-cut store	▷1 To ply cutting area
◯1 Cut to size	◯1 Cut to size
▷2 To temporary store in mould assembly area	▷2 To temporary store in mould assembly area
◖1 Wait	◖1 Wait
▷3 To painting area	▷3 To painting area
◯2 Painting operation	◯2 Painting operation
▷4 To mould storage area	▷4 To ply storage area
▽2 Storage	▽2 Storage

Now these activities are drawn in place on a scale plan of the work area.

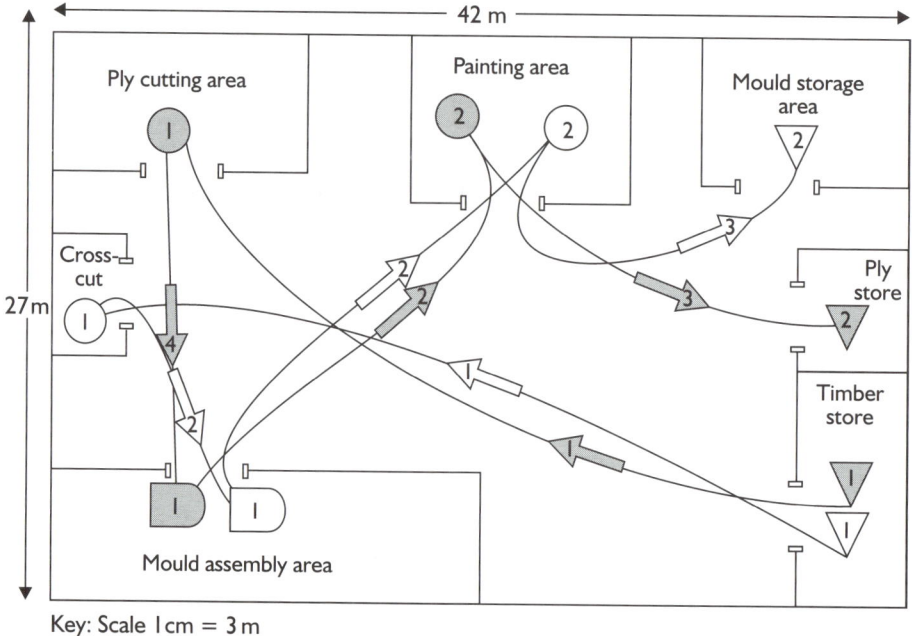

Key: Scale 1 cm = 3 m

34

Session B

Activity 17

2 mins

What do you think is the main advantage of superimposing the flow process chart onto the scaled layout?

Illustrates other potential obstructions / conflicting movements could interrupt the flow.

The answer to this Activity can be found on page 88.

7.2 Other diagrams

There are many variants of the flow diagram, which are used in all kinds of work situations, from recording the movements of a single operator, to kitchen layout design and highway construction.

One example, called a **string diagram**, can be constructed as follows.

- A scale plan of the working area is prepared. This is then attached to a board.
- Pins are inserted in the board at nodes, where:
  - operations are carried out
  - storage takes place
  - delays occur
  - changes in direction occur.
- The end of a length of stiff thread is then attached to the first pin. The thread is wound round the other pins, following the exact route taken in carrying out the process.
- The total length of the thread used, related to the scale of the plan, will give the distance travelled by the materials (or people, information, equipment etc.). Different coloured thread can be used for each person or thing (vehicle, trolley etc.) under study.

This is an effective technique, but has now been largely replaced by computer simulations.

Multiple activity charts are often used when a team is working together on one job. It is constructed in order to record each member's activities on a common timescale.

Session B

8 Examination

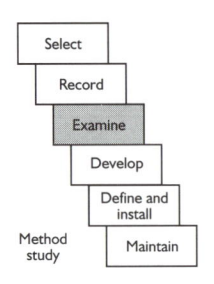

The examination stage starts with a number of telling questions. By questioning, you hope to establish:

- the facts as they are;
- the underlying reasons;
- the alternatives;
- the means by which things can be improved.

Activity 19 (3 mins)

At the 'examine' stage, one question you might ask about a procedure you have recorded is: 'Why is it done in this way?'

Jot down **two** more relevant questions.

Have other ways been tried?
What was the outcome/evaluation of those other ways?

There are many questions you might ask, including:

- 'What is the purpose of the activity?'
- 'Why is it done in this location?'
- 'Why is it done by these particular people?'
- 'Why is it done in this time period?'

We can usefully categorize these questions by separating them into two sets, which we can call **primary questions** and **secondary questions**.

Primary questions concern current methods, and should relate to the following five headings:

- **Purpose**: What is accomplished? Why is it necessary?
- **Means**: How is it done? Why in this way?
- **Place**: Where is it done? Why here?
- **Sequence**: When is it done? Why at this time?
- **Person**: Who does it? Why this person?

Session B

The purpose of the secondary questions is to try to propose alternative methods and to select the best of these alternatives. The options are first listed:

- What **alternative purposes** are there?
- What **alternative means** are there?
- What **alternative places** are there?
- What **alternative sequences** are there?
- What **alternative people** are there?

Then the best of these alternatives is chosen.

9 Development

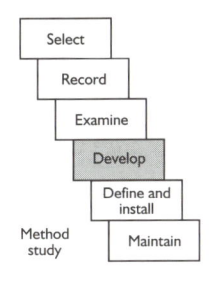

The secondary questions trigger the development stage, which will result in a new method being selected from the proposed alternatives.

Improvement to an existing work process could be brought about by, for instance:

- eliminating a redundant activity;
- modifying an activity;
- combining two or more activities;
- changing the location of the work;
- altering the sequence of activities;
- simplifying the means of doing the work.

10 Definition and installation

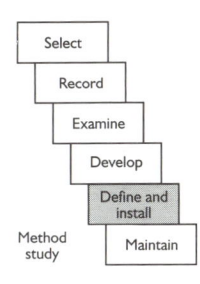

When the investigation has been completed, it is necessary to describe the proposed new work method in detail. This is to enable:

- the method to be installed;
- training and instruction to be given;
- a reference to be provided, in case of any disputes or misunderstandings, and when further changes are being considered.

Anyone investigating a problem or work area should have consulted the people involved at every stage. Installation will certainly be made more difficult if the full co-operation of those affected is not obtained.

Often it is simply not possible to switch suddenly and completely from one method of working to another.

Session B

Activity 20

3 mins

Suppose you have investigated the wages department of a company. After recording the old method of paying wages, you propose a new one, involving new computers and software. Your recommendation is accepted and you are given the go-ahead to order the equipment and install the new system.

*Jot down **two** problems you would have to plan to deal with at this stage.*

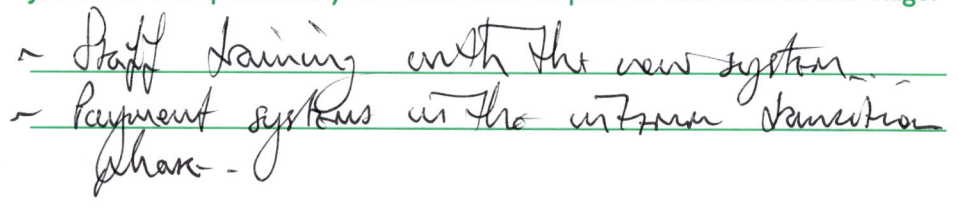

— Staff training with the new system
— Payment systems in the interim transition phase

Your problems might include the questions of:

- how to pay the wages while the new system is being introduced: should the old system continue to run until the new one is completely proven?
- how to train the staff on the new system while it is being installed, and while they are trying to do their own jobs;
- where to find the space to install the new equipment, while the old system is still operational;
- having persuaded the management that the new system will be an improvement, how to persuade the people (and perhaps their union representatives) working on the old one – who may be quite happy with it.

Installing a new method, system or procedure may require a great deal of planning. This stage should really be considered very early on in the project, if the difficulties are to be overcome easily.

11 Maintenance

Once the new method is installed and is working properly, suitable controls should be introduced to ensure that:

- new problems are overcome as they arise;
- improvements are maintained;
- a regular system of feedback is established to monitor performance, targets and quality;
- appropriate modifications are introduced, to deal with changing conditions;
- necessary paperwork actually aids the new method and does not hinder it.

40

Session B

Activity 21

2 mins

Perhaps you will agree that, over a period of time, agreed procedures and practices tend to be altered. From your experience of controlling work activities, what are the reasons why people tend to move away from prescribed methods? Try to list **two** reasons.

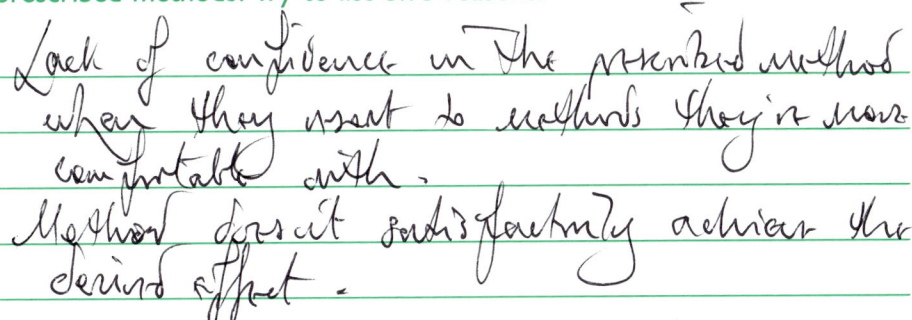

[Handwritten response:]
Lack of confidence in the prescribed method when they resort to methods they're more comfortable with.
Method doesn't satisfactorily achieve the desired effect.

You may agree that people tend to alter their ways of doing things, whether consciously or unconsciously, because:

- the agreed method does not achieve the results required. For example, a procedure that says: 'Cut the 5 metre pipe into 4 equal lengths of 1.25 metres.' might be impractical because it doesn't allow for the material lost during the cutting operation.
- the method may make the job rather awkward or tedious. Most people will tend to do work in the way that is most comfortable for them.
- circumstances change, so that the method needs to be modified.

Maintaining an installed method means making sure

- the method actually works in the way you think it does;
- the people involved are happy and comfortable with it;
- it is modified, in a controlled fashion, to deal with changing conditions;
- that management or those who commissioned or sanctioned the study are happy that the project objectives have been met.

That completes our review of method study techniques. Now we move on to the other aspect of work study: work measurement.

Session B

12 Work measurement

Imagine the following situation.

- You have started up a factory making (say) emergency and first-aid packs. You started off in quite a small way but have become fairly successful, and are now taking on a number of new staff.

You have to keep your costs to a minimum, as you have very little to play with in the pricing of your products. Some of your problems are that:

- you want to pay your employees a bonus for meeting production targets, but don't know at what rate these bonuses should be set;
- you need to know what your costs are very precisely, including the time taken to carry out each task in the manufacturing process;
- you need to know how many product items can be produced each week;
- some method study investigations have been carried out, resulting in proposals for new methods of working; you now need to be able to compare these new methods with existing ones.

Managers are frequently faced with problems like these. To run a business – or any other kind of organization – successfully, it is seldom good enough to rely on broad-brush estimates: precise information is needed.

This is where work measurement can be useful.

Work measurement is defined as the use of techniques to establish how long it takes a qualified worker to do a specified job to a defined level of performance.

Work measurement enables **standards** to be set so that:

- different methods for doing a job can be compared;
- work can be organized so as to achieve optimum results using the available resources;
- incentive schemes can be reasonable and fair;
- defined cost levels can be established;
- realistic planning and estimating can be done for the future.

Work measurement is a well-established technique for providing precise information about the length of time to do a job. It is an important aid in increasing efficiency because it enables management to make accurate calculations, and enables proposed new methods to be compared.

We will take a very brief look at the following work measurement techniques:

- time study
- activity sampling
- predetermined motion time system (PMTS).

Session B

12.1 Time study

This is probably the best known and most widely used technique. It involves the recording of the times and rates of working for clearly identified short elements of a job, usually by direct observation. A stopwatch or an electronic timing device is used.

The stages of time study are as follows.

- Select the job to be studied

    Ideally, **method study** should have already been applied to the job. There's no point in measuring work which is known to use inefficient procedures.

- Break down the job into short parts or phases called **elements**

    Elements are short distinct tasks (such as tightening a screw, or moving an item from one location to another). It is important that each element is separately recognisable. Normally jobs are broken down into elements which take no more than half a minute to complete.

- record the activity to obtain the **observed time** for each element

    There are several difficulties attached to observation, not the least of which is that people tend to behave differently when they are being watched.

- calculate the **standard time** for the job

    These calculations are discussed below.

Let's take an example: a road tanker holding chemicals being unloaded into a storage tank. First, the job is selected and described; all the equipment listed. The operation might be described as:

> 'Tanker Off-Loading Operation for MEG. Section C6. Tanker loaded with Monoethylene Glycol in place at off-loading bay. Operator provided with full protective clothing: PVC gloves, goggles, helmet, boots. Pump zeroed. Hoses on gantry.'

Session B

The job is then broken down into elements. The sheet listing these elements might look like the following:

Element breakdown	Operation or Job	Reference
WS Officer: J. Perks	Tanker off-loading operation for MEG	Section C6 Date 25/8/95

Element No	Description of elements with breakpoint
1	Inform plant foreman of commencement of operation by using the telephone handset provided. Breakpoint: telephone handset replaced.
2	Visually inspect storage tank has adequate capacity to receive load. Operator notes reading on gauge. Breakpoint: operator returns to bottom of gantry steps.
3	Check that import line storage valves to other storage tanks are closed. Operator physically checks to ensure that valves are turned fully clockwise. Breakpoint: operator arrives to open correct valve.

Once the observations start, the length of time for each element is recorded.

Interruptions to the work may occur – such as the employee waiting for work instructions, stopping to chat with a colleague and so on. The work study officer would record all these as 'ineffective time' so that they are taken into account when rating the job.

The observations and timing of elements will normally continue until the officer has enough data. Now, for each element, observed times and standard ratings have to be converted to standard times.

Let's look now at what is meant by these terms: observed times, standard ratings and standard times.

So that different jobs can be compared, work measurement is always made in units of **time**. The time taken to complete any job is the time which a qualified worker would take.

To measure the time for a certain job of work, we observe a skilled operator doing the work and note that he takes 60 minutes to complete the job. This is the **observed time**.	**Observed time** = 60 minutes.

To compare this operator with others, we need to have a standard to work to. This standard is the optimum rate of output that can be achieved by a qualified worker on average over a day or shift: this is known as **standard performance** or **standard rate** of working. It is usually given a rating of 100.

44

Session B

> Assume a second operator actually works faster than the standard rate – in fact he works 25 per cent faster. This means his rate of working is 125, compared with the standard rate of 100. This gives us what is called the **basic time**.

> **Basic time** =
>
> $$\text{Observed time} \times \frac{\text{Observed rating}}{\text{Standard rating}}.$$
>
> So, for this operator:
>
> **Basic time** = $60 \times \dfrac{125}{100} = 75.$

No one can work non-stop. Everyone needs a break now and then. **Relaxation allowance** is the time agreed, according to the job and the circumstances, so that a worker can attend to personal needs and overcome fatigue.

> Let's suppose that the agreed relaxation allowance for the job we are observing is 10 minutes.

> Basic time + Relaxation allowance = Standard time.
>
> So in this case,
>
> **Standard time** = 75 + 10 = 85.

On top of the relaxation time, a **contingency allowance** may be agreed, if for example, there are small amounts of defective materials. Other allowances may be made for times when machines are coming up to speed.

> On this job, we'll assume that contingency and other allowances come to 2 minutes.

> Standard time + Contingency and other allowances = **Allowed time**.
>
> So for our job,
>
> **Allowed time** = 85 + 2
> = 87 minutes.

The following table summarizes these different times:

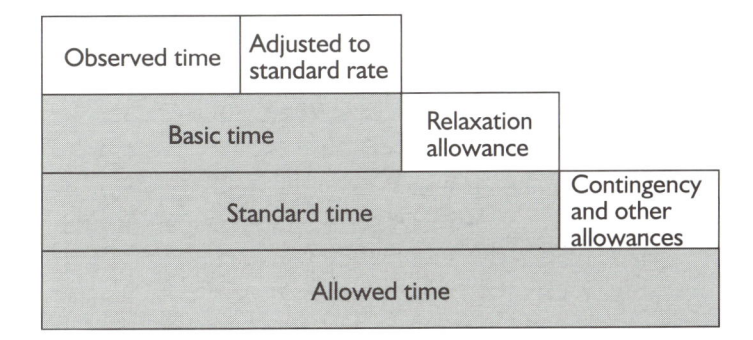

Observed time	Adjusted to standard rate		
Basic time		Relaxation allowance	
Standard time			Contingency and other allowances
Allowed time			

45

Session B

Activity 22

4 mins

On a certain job the observed time is 30 minutes, and the standard rate is set at 100. An operator under observation works 10 per cent faster than the standard rate. There is an agreed relaxation allowance of 6 minutes for the job. In addition, a contingency allowance of 2 minutes is included. What is the allowed time?

Answers to this Activity can be found on page 88.

Allowed time is normally used as a basis for calculations of pay rates, because it is intended to be the standard time to do a job, plus the allowances for breaks and contingencies.

12.2 Activity sampling

Suppose the management of an organization want to find out the percentage of time spent on each one of a number of activities. One obvious way to ascertain this information would be to set up time studies to observe the activities of each person or machine continuously over a period of time. For a large organization the cost of such an exercise would be very high indeed.

An alternative for this – and for other situations where it isn't practicable to spend large amounts of time and effort on continuous observation – is to take **sample** observations.

Let's look at an example.

A machine is being used intermittently. By observing it continuously over a period of one day the following pattern of working is recorded:

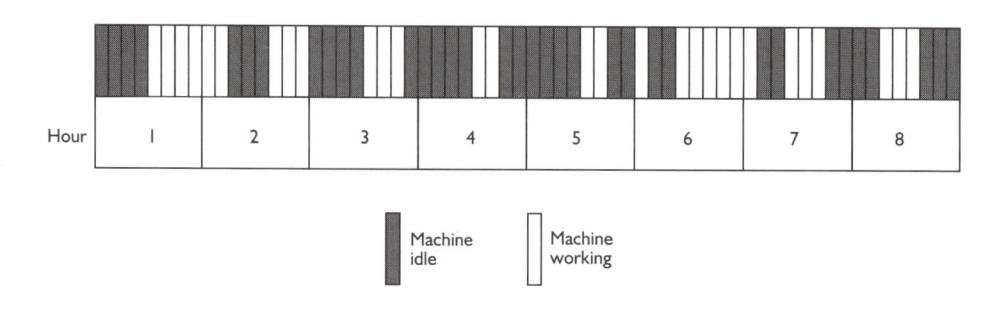

[Diagram showing 8 hours divided into segments, with Machine idle (dark) and Machine working (light) indicators]

On the diagram each hour is divided into eight equal segments. The percentage of time that the machine is idle is calculated as follows:

$$\frac{\text{number of idle segments}}{\text{total number of segments}} \times 100\%$$

Session B

By applying this to the above case, we note that the machine is working for approximately 45.3 per cent of the time, and idle for 54.7 per cent of the time. (You can check this for yourself if you wish.)

Rather than watching the machine continuously, sample observations can be taken. This only entails taking a quick look at the machine at random times throughout the day and recording whether the machine is working or idle. A single observer could go round checking a number of machines in a single day, recording samples for each one.

You can see the idea of sampling in the diagram below:

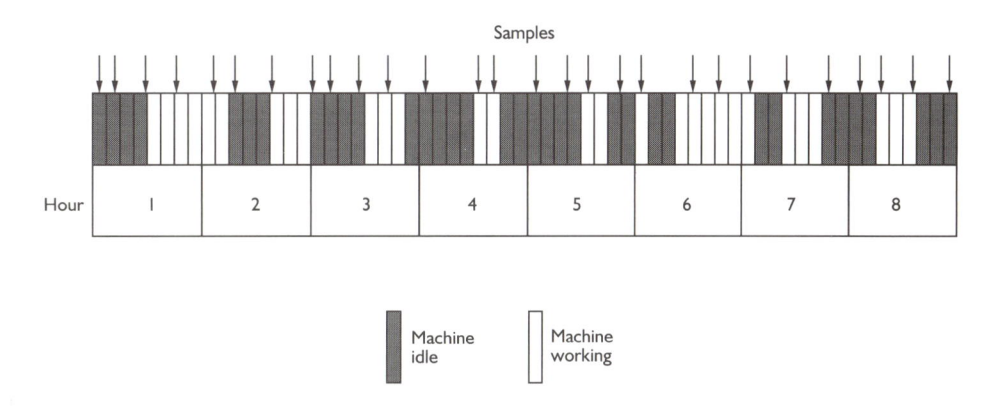

As you can see, 28 sample observations during the day have been taken in this example.

We can now estimate the percentage of idle time by checking the percentage of samples made when the machine was idle.

A total of 14 samples were taken when the machine was idle and 14 taken when the machine was working.

We can therefore estimate the percentage of idle time by dividing the number of 'idle' samples by the total number of samples:

$$\frac{14}{28} = 0.5$$

Multiplying by 100 gives us a figure of 50 per cent. The actual amount of idle time was 54.7 per cent. The estimated amount of idle time was 50 per cent – a difference of 4.7 per cent.

As you might expect, sampling does not give results which are exactly correct.

Session B

Activity 23

How do you think we could improve the accuracy of the result when sampling?

Take more samples

You may have suggested, quite correctly, that the accuracy could be improved by taking more samples. The more samples that are taken, the more accurate the result.

Activity sampling gives reasonably accurate results and is much more economical than full-scale time studies. It can also be used to study operations where accurate timing is not relevant. For instance, it would be possible to study a clerk at work and obtain a good estimate of the average time spent on each of various activities: calculating, writing, filing, keying in a computer terminal and so on.

12.3 Predetermined motion time system (PMTS)

The **predetermined motion time system** (PMTS) identifies specific sets of basic human arm, leg or body motions, for which standard ratings can be applied.

Over the years a number of systems have been developed. One in common use these days is called 'MTM-2'.

In the table on page 49 you can see a summary of the various motions identified in MTM-2. (You don't have to remember these.)

Session B

Category	Class
Get (G): A motion with the predominant purpose of reaching with the hand or fingers to an object, grasping the object, and subsequently releasing it.	GA No grasping motion. GB Grasping motion involving closing of the hand or fingers with one motion. GC Complex grasping motion. GW Get weight: the action required for the muscles of the hand or arm to take up the weight of an object.
Put (P): A motion with the predominant purpose of moving an object to a destination with the hand or fingers.	PA Continuous smooth motion. PB Discontinuous motion, but without obvious correcting motion. PC Discontinuous motion with obvious correcting motions (e.g. stop, hesitation or change in direction).
Apply pressure (A): An action with the purpose of exerting muscular force on an object.	A
Regrasp (R): The hand motion performed with the purpose of changing the grasp of an object.	R
Eye action (E): The action with the purpose of either (a) recognizing a readily distinguishable characteristic of an object, or (b) shifting vision to a new viewing area.	E
Foot motion (F): A short foot or leg motion, the purpose of which is not to move the object.	F
Step (S): Either (a) a leg motion with the purpose of moving the object, or (b) a leg motion longer than 30 cm.	S
Bend and arise (B): Bend, stoop or kneel on one knee and subsequently arise.	B
Crank (C): A motion with the purpose of moving an object in a circular path more than 180° with the hand or fingers.	C

Session B

Extensive experiments and observations have taken place over many years on these basic human motions. The result of all this work is that an average time to perform each action has been identified. This means that there is no need for standard ratings to be applied, because the same times can be used for any operator.

Here are a couple of examples. The unit of time measurement is a TMU (Time Measurement Unit) where 1 TMU = 0.036 seconds.

- the time taken for a 'Get' action (no grasping motion: GA), over a distance of 30 cm is 9 TMUs;
- the time taken for a 'Step' motion (S) is 18 TMUs;
- the time taken for a discontinuous 'Put' motion with correcting motions (PC) over a distance of 45 cm is 36 TMUs.

Activity 24

2 mins

Jot down **one** advantage of PMTS over time study.

Can apply in any job situation.

Answers to this Activity can be found on page 88.

One disadvantage of PMTS is that it requires a lot of training to be able to recognize the correct individual motions in a complex Activity.

13 Some newer techniques

EXTENSIONS 1, 2 AND 3 Benchmarking, continuous improvement and other newer techniques are described in the books listed in these extensions on page 83.

Some of the more recently introduced techniques for improving process efficiency include:

- benchmarking
- continuous improvement.

We will take a quick look at these.

Session B

13.1 Benchmarking

Most go-ahead organizations compare themselves with their competitors. **Benchmarking** is a formal way of comparing a particular process in one organization against the best in the industry (or in the world), and using this knowledge as a basis for improvement.

It consists of the following steps.

- **Selection of the process** to be improved

    Often, processes which cross functions and departments are chosen, on the basis that they are likely to have most room for improvement.

- **Investigation of the process**

    A project team studies and documents the organization's process in detail, perhaps using some of the techniques we have already discussed.

- **Identification of the benchmark**

    An established reference point is needed in the particular business sector concerned; usually this will be a respected competitor. The most productive approach is to collaborate with the organization being used as a benchmark; this can have benefits for both parties, provided there is a strict agreement about confidentiality.

    Alternatively, information about comparative industry standards may be obtainable via external consultants or survey organizations.

- **Comparison with the benchmark**

    Normally the project team will visit the benchmarking organization, having sent a list of detailed questions in advance.

- **Determination of current performance gaps**

    The investigation and comparison is likely to reveal a number of differences between the organization's process and the best practice.

- **Communicate findings and develop improvements**

    Many examples of successes with benchmarking have been reported, for example:

    - Rank Xerox improved its photocopier product development process, after comparing it with Japanese firms in the same industry.
    - ICL improved its training methods after benchmarking them against those of Royal Mail.
    - A US airline compared its aircraft turnaround processes with techniques used in motor racing pit stops.

Session B

13.2 Continuous improvement

EXTENSIONS 1, 2 AND 3
The subject of TQM is covered in the books listed in these extensions on page 83.

Continuous (or continual) improvement is more of a philosophy or culture than a project. As its name suggests, the purpose is to identify and implement ways of doing things better, on a continuous basis.

It is really a facet of **Total Quality Management (TQM)**. When an organization adopts the TQM approach, quality is no longer the function of a single department, but is the responsibility of every department and every individual. It embraces all aspects of the firm's business.

Whereas **continuous improvement** is set up and supported by management, it is really at the lower levels of the organization where initiatives are looked for. Under this system, workteams, working for front-line managers, are given training in process improvement techniques, such as:

- brainstorming
- problem identification and solving
- team working
- statistical techniques.

Once trained, workteams are encouraged to:

- analyse the processes they work with
- document them
- identify areas for improvement
- put forward ideas
- implement the ideas, if necessary carrying out trials or experiments beforehand.

When one project is complete, it is publicized within the organization, and a new project begins.

Activity 25 (3 mins)

Suggest **two** or **three** advantages of continuous improvement.

Applies to everyone in the team
Everyone therefore makes a contribution
Everyone has ownership of any improvements made.

Session B

From what you understand of continuous improvement, perhaps you would agree that it is likely to have the effect of:

- gradually improving work processes;
- motivating workteam members, who feel involved in what they are doing, and empowered to control their own work processes;
- generating a culture of awareness of efficiency and quality
- increasing profits for the organization.

Of course, the biggest gains in improvement tend to come when the scheme is first introduced.

14 Efficiency and effectiveness of 'white collar workers'

Perhaps you have 'white collar' or 'non-productive' workers in your workteam. Obviously, the efficiency and effectiveness of these staff cannot be reduced to simple equations.

There are a whole range of white collar workers, from those who perform routine tasks, such as junior clerks, through to 'knowledge workers', who earn their living by applying expert knowledge.

It is usually easier and more realistic to assess the overall performance or **effectiveness** of a lawyer, engineer, accountant, or other professional person, than his or her efficiency. The abilities of a barrister who impresses in the court-room, and wins lots of cases, will be readily recognized. Similarly, an information specialist will be respected if he or she is able to give advice that solves problems and saves money.

Sometimes it is more appropriate to measure performance at the group level.

Activity 26 (2 mins)

For example, suppose you are a member of a project team assigned to manage a new service planned by a building society. You work together in a team consisting of financial experts, customer service specialists, and marketing consultants. Your aim is to design the product from a basic specification and see it through its launch.

How do you think your work will be assessed?

Ease of introduction, success of outcomes as a result of new service, contribution to rest of team

Session B

Perhaps you will agree that the work of any product development team will be judged on the marketing success of the product: in this case the reactions of the financial press, the interest shown by the public, and (in particular) the numbers sold.

If one of the workteam is inefficient or ineffective, it may mean that the others in the group have to work harder, or else risk the success of the project. If the workteam's objectives are achieved, every member of the workteam will be associated with that accomplishment; if they are not, all will tend to be 'tainted' with failure.

In the example we've just looked at, where a defined project is involved, success is measured by **what is accomplished**.

In other cases, this criterion cannot be used. For instance, if the team:

- produces no easily identifiable outputs, such as a group giving help and advice to people in the community; or
- has a fluctuating membership – as in, for example, a long project involving a number of managers and consultants over a period of time;

it will be more difficult to measure the extent of success of the group.

Instead, we must judge teams and individuals on **how the work is done**.

> **EXTENSION 3**
> This list has been taken from *Operations Management* by Roger G. Schroeder.

One list of measures which has been devised is the following:

- **Degree of innovation**

  Creativity, and the ability to develop and implement new ideas is desired. In assessing innovation, the sort of question that might be asked: 'How many new ideas has this person come up with, that had a successful outcome?'

- **Handling of non-standard situations**

  Knowledge workers do not carry out the kind of routine work that work study is designed to measure. Instead, they must regularly cope with new situations.

- **Degree of immersion in the job**

  A knowledge worker's degree of immersion will be a measure of his or her motivation. This could be said to be a measure of effort or efficiency, but enthusiasm does not always imply effectiveness.

- **Meeting of deadlines**

  This is another efficiency measure. An innovator is not necessarily good at working to a strict schedule.

- **Lack of surprises**

  This is important in some jobs.

Session B

Activity 27 (2 mins)

Explain briefly why 'lack of surprises' might be considered an important quality in a knowledge worker.

Surprises can disrupt the smooth flow of production.

This term, as you may have guessed, is in many ways a measure of discipline. Someone who does not keep others informed of progress will spring surprises, which may result in making the work of colleagues (and perhaps customers) more difficult.

- **Documentation and transferability of work**

This can be crucial in some work environments. Perhaps the most obvious case is that of computer programmers, whose work may be impossible to be understood by others unless it is fully documented.

- **Adaptability to change**

Those who struggle to adjust to change hold up their colleagues, and rarely survive long in their jobs.

Self-assessment 2 (10 mins)

1. The inputs to some process cost £2500, and the outputs are valued at £4500. Five people are employed on the process. Work out the overall productivity, and the output per head.

    $\frac{4500}{2500} = 1.8 \qquad \frac{4500}{5} = £900$

2. Match each of the descriptions with the correct term from the list below.

    a Aiming to identify and implement ways of doing things better, on a continuous basis. *Continuous improvement*
    b Formally comparing a particular process in an organization against the best in the industry. *Benchmarking*
    c Identifying specific sets of basic human arm, leg or body motions, for which standard ratings can be applied. *PMTS*
    d Observing a process or activity at irregular intervals, in order to estimate the percentage of time that it is in a certain state or condition. *Activity sampling*
    e Systematically recording the way work is done, followed by analysis and development of the new methods, with the aim of doing the work better. *Method study*

Session B

    f Aiming to analyse work methods, and the materials and equipment used, in order to: determine the most economical way of doing the work; standardize the method, and install it as standard practice; establish the time required by a qualified and trained worker to carry out the job, at a defined level of performance. *Work study*

    g Systematically measuring the time it takes a skilled person to do a job of work, so as to compare methods and set realistic rates and schedules. *Work measurement*

ACTIVITY SAMPLING   PMTS
BENCHMARKING   WORK MEASUREMENT
CONTINUOUS IMPROVEMENT WORK STUDY
METHOD STUDY

3   The steps of method study have become muddled up in this diagram. Put them in the correct order.

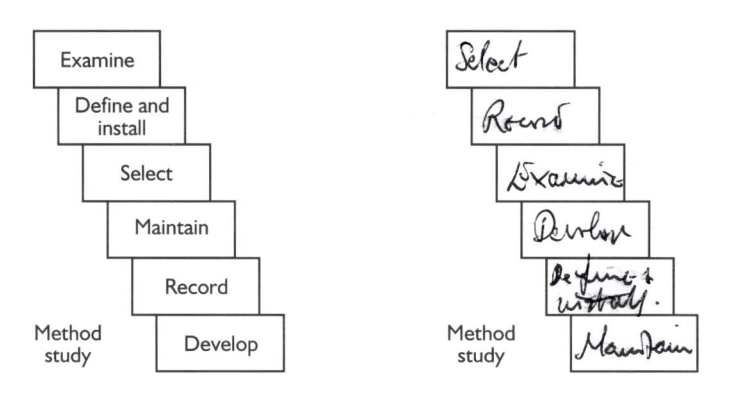

Handwritten answer: Select, Record, Examine, Develop, Define & install, Maintain

4   Identify each of the symbols used in process chart recording by matching it with the correct name on the right.

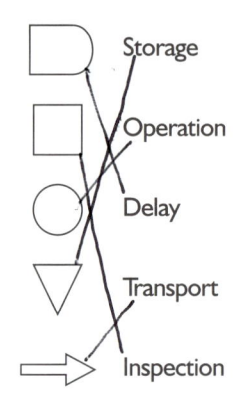

Matching: D-shape → Storage; Square → Operation; Circle → Inspection; Triangle → Delay; Arrow → Transport

Answers to these questions can be found on pages 85–6.

15 Summary

- Productivity is expressed as a ratio of what we get out for what we put in, i.e.

$$\frac{\text{output}}{\text{input}}$$

Productivity rises if the output is increased without increasing the input, or if the output stays the same but the input is decreased.

- Work study, comprising method study and work measurement, aims to analyse work methods, and the materials and equipment used, in order to:
  - determine the most economical way of doing the work;
  - standardize the method, and install it as standard practice;
  - establish the time required by a qualified and trained worker to carry out the job, at a defined level of performance.

- Method study is the systematic recording of the way work is done, followed by analysis and development of the new methods, with the aim of doing the work better.

- Work measurement is the systematic measurement of the time it takes a skilled person to do a job of work, so as to compare methods and set realistic rates and schedules.

- Method study consists of the following steps:
  - Select the problem or work area to be studied.
  - Record what is actually taking place at the moment.
  - Examine and analyse what has been recorded and find out any inefficiencies or shortcomings in existing methods.
  - Develop alternatives to existing methods which are both new and improved.
  - Define and install the new method(s).
  - Maintain the newly installed method(s), to make sure they have achieved the required level of efficiency.

- Method study recording techniques include process charts, flow process diagrams, string diagrams and multiple activity charts.

- In work measurement:
  - allowed time = standard time + contingency and other allowances;
  - standard time = basic time + relaxation allowance;
  - basic time = observed time, adjusted to standard rate.

- Activity sampling consists of observing a process or activity at irregular intervals, in order to estimate the percentage of time that it is in a certain state or condition.

Session B

- Predetermined motion time system (PMTS) comprises the identification of specific sets of basic human arm, leg or body motions, for which standard ratings can be applied.

- Benchmarking is a formal way of comparing a particular organization's process against the best in the industry (or the world) and using this knowledge as a basis for improvement.

- Continuous improvement is a facet of Total Quality Management (TQM) in which the aim is to identify and implement ways of doing things better, on a continuous basis.

- White collar workers may be assessed either on what is accomplished (as an individual or a group), or how the work is done. One list of measures consists of the:
  - degree of innovation;
  - handling of non-standard situations;
  - degree of immersion in the job;
  - meeting of deadlines;
  - lack of surprises;
  - documentation and transferability of work;
  - adaptability to change.

Session C Efficiency in your workplace

1 Introduction

> You should note that, although this session is shorter than the last, it contains a number of Activities which may involve you in several hours of work.

- Terry Wisham, the Chief Executive of Clairbuoys Ltd, attended a presentation by one of his managers on the application of work study techniques to some of the organization's methods. He listened with interest, but gave a guarded response.

  'OK. Supposing we spend several weeks of valuable time recording and measuring,' he said, 'working out exactly how long it should take to perform these tasks, what then? What I'm interested in is in finding efficiency improvements that are real and lasting.'

These techniques, which you read about in the last session, are useful and interesting. However, they are not magic formulae, which will lead to efficiency enhancements automatically. They are practical tools which are intended to be used with careful thought and planning. If and when you do apply them, it may not be entirely apparent how they will help you in your search for increased efficiency. So what's the best approach?

You will recall that we noted in Session A that **it is in the management of resources that the key to efficiency lies**. It is therefore the aim of this final session to help you identify:

- the resources you have;
- ways of planning for saving on these resources.

Session C

2 What resources do you have?

We know that maintaining and improving efficiency consists of making the best use of available resources. Now it's time for you to answer the question:

> In relation to your own job and circumstances, how do you plan to 'make the best use of available resources'?

First, you will need to identify the resources at your disposal.

Let's look at each type of resource in turn.

2.1 People

People (if we agree to use the term!) are a special kind of resource. It could be said that they are the most difficult resource to develop, and, if badly handled, may bring the downfall of the organization. On the other hand,

if you get your team fully motivated and working towards the right objectives, efficiency and effectiveness will follow almost automatically.

Portfolio of evidence B1.1, B1.2

Activity 28

15+ mins

This Activity, together with a later one (Activity 34 on page 67), will provide you with a basis for a structured approach to increasing efficiency, by finding ways to advance the potential of your team.

This Activity may provide the basis of appropriate evidence for your S/NVQ portfolio. Whether or not you decide to do this, you may like to use these two Activities as a basis for a plan of your own; you can come back to them periodically when you are thinking about possible improvements in efficiency.

Use a separate sheet of paper for this Activity.

Write down the names and brief details of your team members. If you feel you know an individual reasonably well, just jot down in brief notes his or her main skills and experience. (Remember, this is for your own benefit, and no one else's.) If you find this difficult, it may be that you need to find out more about the person concerned; in this case, remind yourself of the fact.

Session C

Then try to think of at least one kind of task that you think each person is capable of performing, that he or she does not currently do.

Set out your sheet of paper as follows, repeated for as many people as you have in your team.

Name and main job function	Brief summary of skills and experience
	I need to get to know more about this team member ☐

This person has the potential to:

2.2 Workspace

We listed land and buildings among the main resources of organizations, but when it gets down to individual teams it is more appropriate to talk about workspace.

Portfolio of evidence B1.1, B1.2

Activity 29

10+ mins

This Activity, together with a later one (Activity 35 on page 68), is designed to help you to make optimum use of your workspace.

This Activity may provide the basis of appropriate evidence for your S/NVQ portfolio.

Your next task is to set down on paper (or in a computer if you have suitable software available), the workspace which you are able to use.

It may be appropriate to draw a plan, if your team all work in one area. Alternatively, you could just make a list. Remember that your eventual aim is to find better ways of using your workspace.

(For some managers, for example those who lead teams who are travelling most of the time, or who spend their time on other organizations' premises, this Activity may not be very meaningful. If this is the case with you, ignore it.)

Session C

2.3 Machinery and equipment

These words cover a vast range of 'tools', which obviously varies considerably from one type of job to the next.

Activity 30

Portfolio of evidence B1.1, B1.2

15+ mins

This Activity, together with a later one (Activity 36 on page 69), will provide you with a basis for a structured approach to making better use of your work equipment.

This Activity may provide the basis of appropriate evidence for your S/NVQ portfolio.

The purpose of this Activity is to list the equipment and machinery you and your team have at your disposal. You may find this useful when you want to:

- plan maintenance;
- sell off surplus equipment;
- create more space;
- share resources with other departments;

and so on.

You may decide that there is no point in writing down every individual item: the idea is to remind yourself of the kind of equipment that you have available, and in what numbers.

Again, bear in mind that you will be aiming to find better ways of using your resources. There may be equipment that you under-utilize, for example, or that is in a poor state of repair. Some types of equipment may be badly suited for the task they are used for. As you go through your list, make a note of any points like this that occur to you. Another important question for you to answer is: 'Do we understand how this equipment works?'

Better still, ask some of your team members to make up this list; it is quite possible that their knowledge of the gear and the problems is superior to yours.

One way of setting out an equipment listing is as follows, but your list should be appropriate for your needs.

Item, or equipment type	Approximate numbers available	Uses	Problems/comments

2.1. People Resources

NAME	MAIN JOB FUNCTION	BRIEF SUMMARY OF SKILLS & EXPERIENCES
		POTENTIAL
SK	H of Centre	Broad client group as well as through induction & support for colleagues. Works well with young people.
		Short experience nationally
JS	H of Centre (acting)	Good experience of working with client group + support for colleagues as well as pupils.
		School Support Team @ High School.
JR	Incl. Coord.	Broad with emphasis on exclusion and creating packages.
		LEA rep @ FLS mtgs.
CA	AST	Recent broad experience in High School.
		SST @ High School. Sec. Beh. Forum.
HC	AST	Long experience in KS1/2 & SST/SEN
		Developing KS1/2 curric

JG   AST   Long experience of KS1/2/3 & behaviour problems.

                     Developing curric in Maths

GC   AST   Good experience of KS 3 & High school work.

                     See Beh Forum

LC   AST   Good experience of behaviour across KS's.

                     See Beh Forum

SH   AST   Good experience of KS 1/2 & developing curriculum

                     SST work

2.2   NOT APPLICABLE
2.3   Machinery Equipment

ITEM	NUMBERS AVAILABLE	USED	PROBLEMS/COMMENTS
Photocopier	3 (1 @ each centre)	Staff/pupil	Info required
Computers	Several @ each centre	Staff/pupil copying	Maintenance
Assessment materials	Set @ each centre	Staff with clients	Not enough

✓

Session C

2.4 Materials and components

Now we come to the things that get used up in the transformation process.

Activity 31

Portfolio of evidence B1.1, B1.2

15+ mins

This Activity, together with a later one (Activity 37 on page 70), will provide you with a basis for a structured approach to increased efficiency in the use of materials.

This Activity may provide the basis of appropriate evidence for your S/NVQ portfolio.

In a similar manner to your listing of equipment in Activity 30, identify the materials and components that are the inputs to your team's work process, together with any consumables.

This time, it might be relevant to also note down your current wastage rate for each item, if you know it. (There may be a number of reasons why wastage occurs, apart from spoiled material. For example, a team servicing computers will need to carry parts, some of which may become outdated before they are used.)

Again, make the list as detailed as you feel is appropriate for your needs. If you are able to write down this list without reference to other sources, a quick summary may be all that's required. But if you are not clear about what kinds of materials are used by your workteam, it could be a good idea to do some research on the subject.

Use a separate sheet of paper as before.

2.5 Energy

The amount of energy your team uses can be measured by your fuel utilization. The difficulty with identifying this resource is that, typically, electricity and other forms of fuel will be shared with others in the organization. It is more productive to discuss ways of saving energy, and we'll leave discussion of this resource until later in the session.

Session C

2.6 Time

Time is allocated to everyone equally, and yet is still very precious. Perhaps it is not a good idea to ask you to identify how much time you have to spare, as you may decide to leave the paper blank!

2.7 Finance

The amount of financial responsibility given to team leaders and front-line managers varies considerably. For the next Activity, you are asked to write down the extent of your own authority to handle finances.

Activity 32 · 5 mins

How much scope do you have when it comes to spending the organization's money?

a How large a budget do you control, if any, and what kind of items are you permitted to buy or hire?

Small budget for communication, day to day materials, new materials.

b If you do not have your own budget, how much practical, effective control do you have over the purchase of materials, the hiring of people etc.? (For example, you may not officially be a signatory on documents that authorize the spending of money, but your recommendations may, to some extent, be accepted without question.)

Purchase of materials + hiring of people is centrally controlled.

c To what degree do you feel your efforts are being frustrated by the lack of control you have over finances? Do you think you could make your team more efficient if you were able to make more financial decisions, for example? If so, how could you persuade your manager of this fact?

Lack of control presents difficulties particularly over unsuitables which can't be budgeted for on a limited budget.

Session C

2.8 Information

This is the last item on our list of resources. Sources and types of information are many and varied, and are therefore difficult to summarize. Instead, you are asked to identify deficiencies.

Activity 33

Portfolio of evidence B1.1, B1.2

15+ mins

This Activity, together with a later one (Activity 39 on page 72), will provide you with a basis for a structured approach to increasing efficiency by improving your sources of information.

This Activity may provide the basis of appropriate evidence for your S/NVQ portfolio. If you are intending to take this course of action, it might be better to write your answers on separate sheets of paper.

What kinds of additional information, if any, would help you and your team do your job more efficiently? Answer the following questions by encircling your response and explaining it briefly.

a Would you or your team work more efficiently if you were given more information about the processes or procedures you work with? **Yes**/No

Explain: We have that information – it's when the processes and procedures are compromised that problems arise.

b Would you or your team work more efficiently if you were given more information about the activities of other teams or other parts of the organization? **Yes**/No

Explain: We have a good grasp of what other teams are about & its attempts to bend procedures which causes conflicts.

c Is there any other kind of information that would help to make you or your team work more efficiently? **Yes**/No

Explain: It's the clarity about procedures already in place which needs consolidation and wider circulation.

65

Session C

3 Planning for improved efficiency and effectiveness

Now that you have spent some time analysing and identifying the resources that are currently available to you, it is time to start making plans to:

- utilize those resources in a better way;
- obtain additional resources that would help to make you or your team more efficient;
- increase your effectiveness.

We can go through the same categories as before.

3.1 People

There are many approaches to the management task of getting the best from people. The following are a few ideas to add to your own.

- Training

  Often, individuals feel frustrated at not being able to carry out their work as efficiently and effectively as they would like, because they have not been fully trained. Training may consist of specific instructions and guidance regarding a particular process or procedure, such as how to operate a machine, how to use some computer software, or the safest method of evacuating a building. These are the technical skills.

  Your team may also require training in financial, administrative or interpersonal skills.

  But remember, too, that the training needs of your team may have more to do with their lack of understanding of the principles, or the rationale, behind the work they are asked to do, than the development of specific skills. Thinking people want to know more than **how** to do something, they need to know **why**. For example:

  - cooks and chefs need to understand the concepts behind nutrition, as well as cooking methods and recipes;
  - accountants in a manufacturing company will do a better job if they have a good appreciation of the processes they are being asked to cost;
  - health club instructors may improve their performance if they are trained to explain the effects of particular exercises on the body, rather than simply showing visitors how to use gym equipment.

  Training sessions do not need to be expensive, although it is important that they are conducted in a professional manner.

Session C

- Coaching

A coach is someone who aims to get the best out of people: the best efforts, the best achievements, the best ideas.

By coaching you can:

- convey the objectives of the organization and the team, so that everyone works to the same ends and in the same direction;
- create an atmosphere in which the team is encouraged to work out its own solutions to problems, through understanding, not by simply following a rigid set of steps;
- get people to believe in themselves, and their ability to improve their efficiency and effectiveness.

- Empowering and delegating

The modern concept of a manager is primarily as leader – someone who sets out to gain trust, influence and commitment, and is prepared to give respect and power to the team.

It is the team who must get the job done, and it is the leader's role to provide them with the means to do it: to empower them.

Virtually any and every task can be delegated.

Activity 34

Portfolio of evidence B1.1, B1.2

15+ mins

This Activity, together with Activity 28 on page 60, will provide you with a basis for a structured approach to increasing efficiency, by finding ways to advance the potential of your team.

This Activity may provide the basis of appropriate evidence for your S/NVQ portfolio.

In Activity 28, you were asked to make notes about the members of your team. Now you should use your response to decide what actions to take in order to 'get the best from these resources'. Use the following questions to help you make your decisions. Write your answers on separate sheets of paper.

a What training will you arrange for each of your team members, that will help them to become more efficient or effective? Skills training (technical, administrative, financial, interpersonal)? Education, to give greater awareness and understanding?

b How will you start coaching people to achieve their objectives, and to believe in themselves, and their ability to solve their own problems?

c How do you intend to delegate more tasks, and to empower the team to achieve more?

Session C

3.2 Workspace

Badly used workspace can result in:

- **congestion**

    if workstations are too close together, for example;

- **accidents**

    if there is not enough room, corridors aren't clearly marked, or gangways are blocked;

- **inefficient communications**

    when people can't see each other, when there is too much noise, or when too many people have to use the same phone;

- **excessive energy costs**

    when doors and windows are left open, or a building is badly insulated;

- **low production**

    if there are breaks and discontinuities in the flow.

Activity 35

Portfolio of evidence B1.1, B1.2

15+ mins

This Activity, together with Activity 29 on page 61, is designed to help you to make optimum use of your workspace.

This Activity may provide the basis of appropriate evidence for your S/NVQ portfolio.

In Activity 29, you set out the workspace available to your team. In doing so, you may have thought up some ideas of the ways in which you might improve the use of the available space, or some means of acquiring additional space.

Now set up a meeting with your team about this subject. What problems do they see? How would they solve them? (You may be able to delegate this whole task, and take on the role of coach and facilitator.)

Write down the results of your meeting on a separate sheet of paper, and say what your next step will be.

Session C

3.3 Machinery and equipment

Earlier (in Activity 30), you were asked to list the equipment and machinery your team uses, and to identify any problems with it. Now's the time to think about ways of solving those problems, and of utilizing these items more efficiently.

Portfolio of evidence B1.1, B1.2

Activity 36

15+ mins

This Activity, together with Activity 30 on page 62, will provide you with a basis for a structured approach to making better use of your work equipment.

This Activity may provide the basis of appropriate evidence for your S/NVQ portfolio.

Following the work you did in the earlier Activity, you may have pinpointed a number of problems, such as worn or damaged equipment, or machinery not properly understood. You will need now to find ways of helping your workteam solve these problems.

If you haven't done so already, it's probably a good idea to consult your team about this. They may be able to suggest and implement solutions without your intervention.

Get your ideas and problem solutions written down on separate sheets of paper.

Session C

3.4 Materials and components

As already mentioned, there may be a good deal of scope for making savings on materials and components.

Activity 37
Portfolio of evidence B1.1, B1.2
15+ mins

This Activity, together with Activity 31 on page 63, will provide you with a basis for a structured approach to increased efficiency in the use of materials.

This Activity may provide the basis of appropriate evidence for your S/NVQ portfolio.

Following your response to Activity 31, you need now to help the workteam find ways of optimizing the use of the materials and components you use. Prompt responses from your workteam members by posing the following questions:

a How can we reduce wastage of materials and consumables?

b Are the materials and components we use the best ones for the job?

c If the answer to (b) is no, how can we identify and obtain better ones?

d Are the processes we use making the best use of the materials and components?

e If the answer to (d) is no, how can the processes be improved?

f Are our end products what our customers want?

g If the answer to (f) is no, what can we do about it?

2.4 Materials & Components

ITEM	Nos Available	USED	PROBLEMS/CONCERNS
Paper	Reams	Notes Aid-memoires Photocopying	? Wastage ? use in an 'e' age. alternatives to paper commn.

3.1 People

a) PD planning through Performance Management identifying training needs and linking to Service Development Objectives.

b) Identifying with them their objectives and negotiating time scales to realise them opportunities. Monitor progress and capitalise on training and/or experience opportunities.

c) By identifying colleagues who express an interest and to seek 'volunteers' to engage in development opportunities.

3.2 NOT APPLICABLE

3.3 MACHINERY & EQUIPMENT

Photocopiers — identify funding/budget
— seek best deal to meet needs & centres
— look at facilities and where efficiency could be demonstrated in machines.
— check out alternatives linked to computers etc..

3.4 Materials and components
   a) Alternative ways of communicating
      Reminders about wastage.
   b) Other forms of communication and wording.
      Reporting is unavoidable in terms of paper usage.
   c) Links with service systems and how they
      would be improved through a uniform system
      of communication and wording.
   d) No.
   e) Investment in a more standardised system
      across the county.
   f) By and large yes.
   g) Ensuring what we do is a consistent service.

3.5 Energy
   ① Asst management review/update
   ② Check employment of energy saving initiatives
      eg doubling up on transport, insulation in
      buildings, reducing wastage when items not
      actually in use.
   ③ Engage with colleagues in awareness raising
      of energy conservation
   ④ Reminders where savings can be made.
   ⑤ Review existing practice and again in 6 months
      & a year as part of H & Safety review.

Session C

3.5 Energy

The key to efficiency when it comes to energy use is simple: save as much of it as possible.

Activity 38

Portfolio of evidence B1.1, B1.2 — 10+ mins

Use the following checklist to help you find ways of saving energy. (The 'you' in this Activity refers to you personally, or any member of your team.) Tick the boxes.

		Yes	No
a	Do you know how much energy you are using?	☒	☐
b	If not, can you find out and bring it to the attention of the team, so you can monitor improvements?	☐	☐

Explain: _____

c	Do you take trouble to ensure that heating, lights and machinery are switched off when they aren't needed?	☒	☐
d	Is there a proper system of maintenance on boilers and other energy-consuming equipment?	☐	☒
e	Do you keep doors and windows closed during the winter months?	☒	☐
f	Does the building where you work have efficient heat insulation?	☐	☒
g	Do you encourage or reward the saving of energy?	☐	☒

Now give your own ideas for saving energy:

Ensuring through asset management that efficient use is made of energy saving initiatives eg insulation, talking to colleagues about saving energy etc.

Finally, on separate sheets, write down the steps you are going to take to make savings in energy.

Session C

3.6 Finances

An overall measure of efficiency, and the one that accountants and chief executives are inclined to use, is the amount of profit made by the organization this year as compared to last. In simple terms, the input is the amount of money put into the enterprise, and the output is the amount of income; the difference is the profit.

The best way to save money is to become more efficient in the use of your resources.

If you are responsible for a budget, you may need to improve your administration and control procedures. You could perhaps:

- keep better records of expenditure and the use of materials, ensuring they are complete, accurate and accessible;
- ensure you monitor and maintain resources such as equipment and materials in accordance with organizational requirements;
- keep your team members informed of their individual responsibilities for the control of resources;
- ensure that, if you need to make spending decisions which thereby exceed your budget, you refer to your line manager or other relevant authority.

3.7 Information

The next (and last) Activity on the efficient use of resources requires you to plan to find the information you and your team need.

Portfolio of evidence B1.1, B1.2 — **Activity 39** — 10 mins

This Activity, together with Activity 33 on page 65, will provide you with a basis for a structured approach to increasing efficiency by improving your sources of information.

This Activity may provide the basis of appropriate evidence for your S/NVQ portfolio.

In Activity 33 you made notes on the kind of information you think you are lacking in. Now explain how you intend to obtain this additional or alternative information.

Enter into dialogue with strategic managers about changes in policies, procedures and processes & seek clarity about position.

Session C

Self-assessment 3

⏱ 10 mins

1 Fill in the blanks in the following sentences with suitable words chosen from the list below.

a If you get your team fully _motivated_ and working towards the right _objectives_, efficiency and effectiveness will follow almost automatically.

b A _coach_ is someone who aims to get the best out of people: the best _efforts_, the best _ideas_, the best _achievements_.

c It is the _team_ who must get the job done, and it is the _leader_'s role to provide them with the means to do it: to _empower_ them.

d Badly used workspace can result in _accidents_, _congestion_, inefficient _communications_, excessive _energy_ costs or low _production_.

ACCIDENTS   EFFORTS   MOTIVATED
ACHIEVEMENTS   EMPOWER   OBJECTIVES
COACH   ENERGY   PRODUCTION
COMMUNICATIONS   IDEAS   TEAM
CONGESTION   LEADER

2 List **four** ways to save energy for someone who works in an office.

- Switch off machines when not in use.
- Gather together several items and move in one go rather than individually.
- Close windows when heating is on in winter.
- Switch off lights.

3 Make **three** suggestions for controlling finances better, for someone who controls a budget for a small department.

- Inspect reports of expenditure & cash flow.
- Ensure staff are aware of responsibilities for control of budget.
- Monitor and maintain resources carefully.

Answers to these questions can be found on page 86.

73

Session C

4 Summary

This session has mainly consisted of suggestions and Activities designed to help you and your workteam become more efficient and effective. Among the questions posed were the following.

- Is your use of people efficient and effective? Are they:
  - trained to perform their assigned tasks;
  - enabled to develop their skills;
  - empowered to take control of their work?

- Could you delegate more tasks?

- Are you, the manager, acting as a leader who not only sets out to gain trust, influence and commitment, but is also prepared to give respect and power to the team?

- How can you utilize your workspace in a more efficient and effective way, so as to avoid:
  - congestion
  - accidents
  - inefficient communications
  - excessive energy costs
  - low levels of production?

- How can you improve your management of equipment and machinery? Is there some that:
  - is under-utilized;
  - is in a poor state of repair;
  - is badly suited for the task it is used for;
  - you understand the operation of insufficiently?

- If you are responsible for a budget, how can you improve your administration and control procedures? Could you perhaps:
  - keep better records of expenditure and the use of materials, ensuring they are complete, accurate and accessible;
  - ensure you monitor and maintain resources such as equipment and materials in accordance with organizational requirements;
  - keep your team members informed of their individual responsibilities for the control of resources;
  - ensure that, if you need to make spending decisions which thereby exceed your budget, you refer to your line manager or other relevant authority?

- Would you or your workteam work more efficiently if you were given more information about the processes or procedures you work with?

- Would you or your workteam work more efficiently if you were given more information about the activities of other teams or other parts of the organization?

- Is there any other kind of information that would help to make you or your workteam work more efficiently?

Performance checks

1 Quick quiz

Jot down the answers to the following questions on *Improving Efficiency*.

Question 1 What three kinds of transformations did we identify?

Improving
Conducting
Transforming

Question 2 What **four** main types of resource did we identify?

People
Materials
Capital
Information

Question 3 Define 'efficiency'.

Making best use of resources in production.

Question 4 Explain the link between effectiveness and organizational objectives.

Agreed objectives have to be met by groups or individuals within service/company/team

Question 5 Express, in your own words, the meaning of 'quality'.

Characteristics of a product that meets needs of the customer.

Question 6 What is meant by 'goodwill', and where does it fit in our categories of resources?

Reputation and credibility as a capital resource.

Question 7 Explain, in your own words, the purpose of method study.

Observing and recording the way a job is done.

Performance checks

Question 8 List the **six** steps of method study.

Select
Record
Examine
Develop
Define + install
Maintain

Question 9 What kind of chart or diagram would be used for recording activities involving the flow analysis of people, information, materials or equipment?

Flow chart demonstrating the process.

Question 10 What, in brief, is a string diagram used for?

Distance travelled in the course of completing a task.

Question 11 Give a definition of work measurement.

Skilled worker completing a task in a given length of time.

Question 12 In time study, what are elements?

Components that make up an overall task.

Question 13 In time study, how does 'allowed time' relate to 'basic time'?

Basic time + relaxation time + contingency time.

Question 14 Explain what 'predetermined motion time system' is, and what it's used for.

Human motions to which standard times can be applied.

Question 15 What is 'benchmarking'?

Comparing performance against the 'best' and using info to improve performance.

Answers to these questions can be found on page 89.

76

Workbook Assessment

1. - Lack of training of operators in the loading process
   - Old and outdated or poorly maintained equipment
   - Lack of appropriate procedures/systems for loading which have been reviewed and monitored.
   - Lack of supervision.

2. Appropriateness of procedures/systems could be investigated through 'method study' together with a string diagram to look at movement in loading process.

3. - Too long personal needs 'breaks'
   - Not taking most direct routes
   - No account having been taken of 'standard times' for journeys and monitoring of actual journey times and reasons for delay.

4. - Check on time for breaks - give guidance on standard reasonable times
   - Monitoring of routes - giving guidance on standard routing since, presumably, traffic flows are fairly consistent.
   - Lay down 'standard' or 'allowed time' which takes into consideration journey time + relaxation and allows for contingency where traffic delays inevitably may occur.

✓

Performance checks

2 Workbook assessment

(60 mins)

Read the following case incident, and then deal with the questions which follow. Write your answers on a separate sheet of paper.

- The management of the Sawbridge Timber and Frame Company would like to improve efficiency in the loading and transport of timber.

  Desmond White, one of their managers, is assigned to carry out an investigation of the problems in this area, and to propose a way forward. He is given authority to recommend any steps he believes are necessary, provided he is able to justify the expense.

  After conducting a preliminary survey, Desmond notes down two points as being the main problems resulting in inefficiency.

  a Lorries are loaded by fork-lift truck. The process is slow, and there have been a number of incidents in which timber was damaged while being loaded. In one case, the cab of a lorry was crushed by falling timber, the driver fortunately not being in the cab at the time.
  b During transport, average journey times seem to be longer than Desmond would have expected.

In answering the following questions, you do not need to write more than a total of a page or so.

1   Suggest **four** possible reasons for the apparent slow and poor handling of timber during the loading process.

2   Assume that, in turn, each one of the four possible reasons listed in (1) is the actual problem. Explain briefly your ideas for finding a solution to this problem.

3   Suggest **three** possible reasons for the long journey times during transport.

4   Assume that, in turn, each one of the three possible reasons listed in (3) is the actual problem. Explain briefly your ideas on finding a solution to this problem.

77

Performance checks

3 Work-based assignment

Portfolio of evidence B1.1, B1.2

60 mins

The time guide for this assignment gives you an approximate idea of how long it is likely to take you to write up your findings. You will find you need to spend some additional time gathering information, talking to colleagues, and thinking about the assignment.

Your written response to this assignment may provide the basis of appropriate evidence for your S/NVQ portfolio. The assignment is also designed to help you to demonstrate your ability to support the efficient use of resources, by:

- obtaining the commitment of others;
- analysing and conceptualizing, by showing that you can think clearly and objectively about the past, and to apply your thinking to present and future plans;
- teambuilding;
- focusing on results;
- making decisions.
- showing your commitment to excellence.

What you have to do

In Session C, you should have begun work on a number of Activities designed to help you plan for the increased efficiency of your workteam and work area. The relevant activities were:

People: Activity 28 on page 60, and 34 on page 67.

Workspace: Activity 29 on page 61, and 35 on page 68.

Equipment: Activity 30 on page 62, and 36 on page 69.

Materials: Activity 31 on page 63, and 37 on page 70.

Information: Activity 33 on page 65, and 39 on page 72.

For this assignment, you are asked to take **one** of these five resource items, and develop your plan to the point of recommending specific changes, which you can reasonably expect to result in real improvements in efficiency.

Present your work in the form of a memorandum addressed to your manager. You will need to give an account of the work you carried out during your investigations, and a justification of any proposed expenditure involved.

So that your tutor can assess your submission, you may need to also provide some brief background information: any relevant details that a non-employee couldn't be expected to know.

Reflect and review

1 Reflect and review

Now that you have completed your work on *Improving Efficiency*, let us review our workbook objectives.

■ You should be better able to explain what is meant by efficiency, and its context in relation to the resources and work processes you manage.

Defining the word 'efficiency' is not difficult. The definition we used was: 'making the best use of resources, to achieve production of goods or services'. What is more relevant is how **you** view efficiency, now that you have finished the workbook, in relation to **your** resources and work processes.

Try to explain what you have learned, by answering the following questions.

■ What inefficiencies have you identified in the way you and your team operate?

Built in time delays for decision making being deferred to meetings scheduled.

■ What are the effects of these inefficiencies on the organization as a whole?

Slowing down the service offer to pupils.

■ You should be better able to describe the principles and purpose of work study, and summarize other techniques designed to improve efficiency and effectiveness.

You may not want to claim that you have become a work study expert as a result of reading this workbook, but you should have a better understanding of the techniques which might be available to you. All of these (work study, benchmarking and so on) require the full commitment of higher management, and you would no doubt need to obtain approval before introducing any of them in your area.

Reflect and review

- Which of the techniques described in Session C do you feel would be useful in your work situation?

  Techniques which revolve around consideration of efficient use of human resources.

- How might you go about investigating the subject further?

  Systematic observation and 'method study' of the way work is done or decisions are made.

■ You should be better able to plan for the best use of resources assigned to you.

We spent a lot of time discussing resources. The Activities you tackled in Session C should have helped you to make plans to use the resources you have more efficiently.

As you should already have made some effort at developing resource plans, you might like now to consider the following two questions.

- Are your resources adequate for your team's needs?

  No — need to plan carefully acquisition of new materials and equipment through asset management planning.

- What new approaches to resource efficiency can you think of?

  Speeding up process of decision making and implementation.

■ You should be better able to contribute effectively to the control of your organization's resources.

Efficiency involves controlling resources as well as planning for their best use. By reducing materials waste, for example, or using equipment to its full potential, you are controlling them, and saving your organization money in doing so.

- Which types of resource do you feel you do **not** have under adequate control?

  None

Reflect and review

3 Extensions

Extension 1

Book   Operations Management
Author   John Naylor
Edition   1996
Publisher Pitman

This book covers a number of the subjects of this workbook, including efficiency and effectiveness, transformation processes, work study, benchmarking, Total Quality Management, and continuous improvement. Particular chapters relevant to our subject are: Chapter 6 – Studying work; Chapter 8 – Facility layout: manufacture and isolated service; Chapter 9 – Facility layout: personal and self service.

As the Preface says: 'This book gives a comprehensive coverage of operations management for those who come to the subject for the first time.'

Extension 2

Book   Essentials of Production and Operations Management
Author   Ray Wild
Edition   Fourth edition, 1995
Publisher Cassell

This reliable book is at an introductory level. It includes case studies from around the world. Specific parts you may want to look at are: Part 4 – Work and Work Systems; Part 6 – Operations Scheduling; Part 8 – The Control of Operating Systems.

Extension 3

Book   Operations Management – Decision Making in the Operations Function
Author   Roger G Schroeder
Edition   Fourth edition, 1993
Publisher McGraw-Hill International Editions

This is an American book, but has been written for an international audience. It is intended as an introductory course for schools of business administration. Associated software can be purchased. Some relevant chapters are: Chapter 4 – Managing Quality; Chapter 5 – Quality Control and Improvement; Chapter 9 – Process-Flow Analysis; Chapter 19 – Managing the Work Force; Chapter 21 – Performance Measurement and Improvement.

These extensions can be taken up via your NEBS Management Centre. They will either have them or will arrange that you have access to them. However, it may be more convenient to check out the materials with your personnel or training people at work – they may well give you access. There are other good reasons for approaching your own people; for example, they will become aware of your interest and you can involve them in your development.

Reflect and review

4 Answers to self-assessment questions

Self-assessment 1
page 20

1 The complete diagram is:

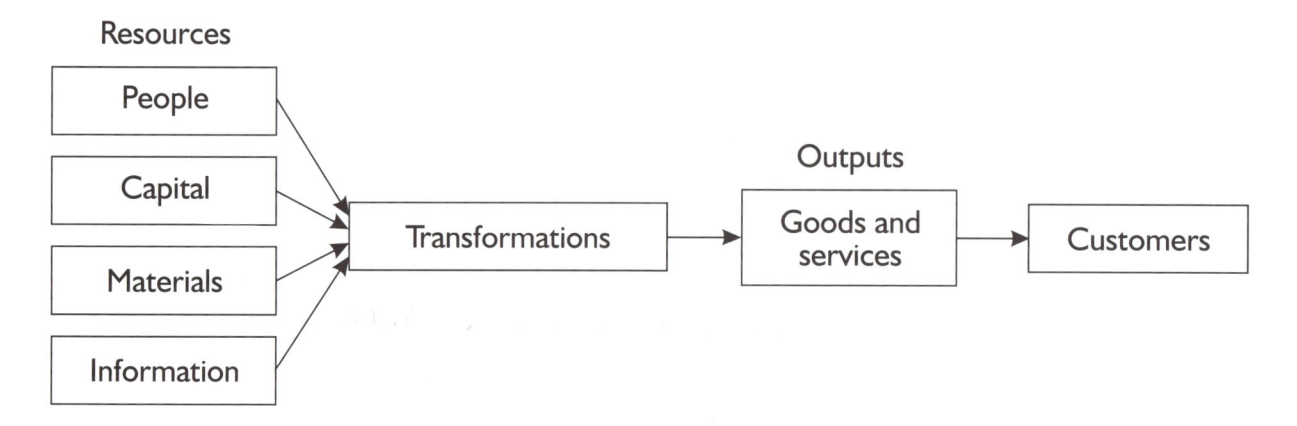

Resources: People, Capital, Materials, Information → Transformations → Outputs: Goods and services → Customers

2 Compare your responses with the answer given below.

Transformation type	Sector			
	Manufacturing	Transport	Supply	Service
Improving	f	b	b	c, e
Caretaking	f	b	b	e
Transferring		a, b	a, b, d	

There may be some here which you disagree with.

a The regional electricity company transfers electricity from the National Grid to its customers. It is therefore in the transport and supply business. There is a case for putting it into the service sector, and you might say that it 'transports' electricity, by providing electricity cables.

b A water company has to purify (i.e. improve) and take care of water, and also transfer it to customers. It is in both the transport and supply business. Again, it might see itself as also providing a service.

c A hairdresser simply provides a hair-improving service.

Reflect and review

    d A hardware shop supplies goods to its customers, but does not improve them or take care of them (except in an incidental way). The shop may also pride itself on the good service it gives.

    e A residential school improves and takes care of children, but does not supply, transport or manufacture them!

    f A farm is a manufacturer, improving, and taking care of crops and farm animals and their products.

3 a EFFICIENCY means making the best use of RESOURCES, to achieve production of goods or SERVICES.

    b Work organizations TRANSFORM resources (capital, materials and INFORMATION, with the help of PEOPLE) into goods and services, which are provided to their CUSTOMERS.

    c QUALITY can be defined as all the FEATURES and characteristics of a product or service that affect its ability to SATISFY the needs of customers and USERS.

    d Loss of GOODWILL comes about through INEFFECTIVENESS or inefficiency, and leads to reduced PROFITS.

Self-assessment 2 page 55

1 The overall productivity is:

$$\frac{\text{output}}{\text{input}} = \frac{4500}{2500} = 1.8$$

The output per head is:

$$\frac{£4500}{5} = £900$$

2 a CONTINUOUS IMPROVEMENT
    b BENCHMARKING
    c PMTS
    d ACTIVITY SAMPLING
    e METHOD STUDY
    f WORK STUDY
    g WORK MEASUREMENT

3 The correct diagram is:

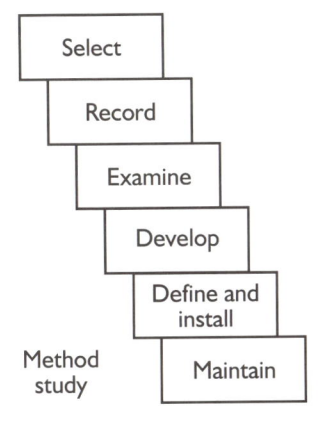

```
                        Select
                          Record
                            Examine
                              Develop
                                Define and
                                install
                    Method       Maintain
                    study
```

Reflect and review

4   The correct names for the symbols are:

○   Operation

□   Inspection

⇨   Transport

⌓   Delay

▽   Storage

Self-assessment 3 page 73

1   a If you get your team fully MOTIVATED and working towards the right OBJECTIVES, efficiency and effectiveness will follow almost automatically.
   b A COACH is someone who aims to get the best out of people: the best EFFORTS, the best ACHIEVEMENTS, the best IDEAS.
   c It is the TEAM who must get the job done, and it is the LEADER's role to provide them with the means to do it: to EMPOWER them.
   d Badly used workspace can result in CONGESTION, ACCIDENTS, inefficient COMMUNICATIONS, excessive ENERGY costs or low PRODUCTION.

2   Ways to save energy in an office could include:

- switching off lights and heating when they aren't needed;
- switching off equipment when it isn't needed;
- keeping doors and windows closed when heating is on;
- getting the building properly insulated.

3   Some suggestions are:

- keep better records of expenditure, ensuring they are complete, accurate and accessible;
- ensure you monitor and maintain resources such as equipment and materials in accordance with organizational requirements;
- keep your team members informed of their individual responsibilities for the control of resources.

Reflect and review

5 Answers to activities

Activity 3 on page 6

You may have noted as people your own workteam, or included other departments such as sales, accounts, shop staff, operators, and so on.

Capital could be the building you work in, the equipment you use in your job, the budgets you work to, or the ground you stand on.

The materials you listed will depend on the kind of work you do; they might be made from paper, metal, plastic, ceramics etc. You may have included gas, electricity or oil as energy consumed.

Information could be in the form of specifications, job descriptions, formulations, reports, and so on.

Activity 5 on page 8

As you may have deduced, the cycle tends to rotate in the opposite direction:

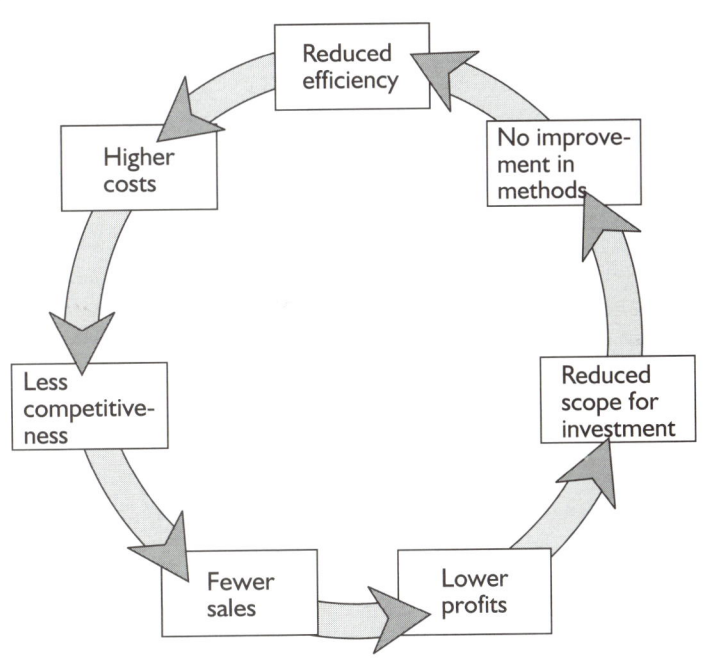

Reduced efficiency → No improvement in methods → Reduced scope for investment → Lower profits → Fewer sales → Less competitiveness → Higher costs → Reduced efficiency

Activity 7 on page 10

It is possible to be **inefficient** by:

- wasting capital, materials or information;
- not using people to their full potential;
- managing transformation processes badly.

Ineffectiveness can be achieved through having:

- the wrong objectives;
- the right objectives, but losing sight of them;
- the right objectives, but getting your plans wrong, so that you are not able to achieve the objectives;
- insufficient or inappropriate resources to implement your plans.

87

Reflect and review

Activity 17 on page 35

The flow process diagram gives a clearer picture of movement, congestion, excess travel, and crowding etc., so is much more useful than a simple flow process chart.

Activity 18 on page 37

One useful item of information which can be obtained from multiple activity charts is the percentage of working time compared with idle or waiting time.

For example, the utilization of Fitter No 1 is calculated as follows:

$$\text{Percentage of time spent working} = \frac{\text{time spent working}}{\text{work cycle}} \times 100\%$$

$$= \frac{440 \text{ secs}}{8 \times 60 \text{ secs}} \times 100\% = 91.7\%$$

Therefore the percentage of time spent waiting = 100% − 91.7% = 8.3%.

Activity 22 on page 46

$$\text{Basic time} = \text{Observed time} \times \frac{\text{Observed rating}}{\text{Standard rating}}$$

So basic time for this operator = $30 \times \frac{110}{100} = 33$

To this we add the relaxation allowance and the contingency allowance

So the allowed time = 33 + 6 + 2 = 41 minutes.

Activity 24 on page 50

The main advantage, as you may agree, is that PMTS can be used in any job situation, and so timings can be transferred from job to job and from organization to organization.

Other advantages are that:

- there is no need to worry about standard ratings;
- the system can be applied to short run tasks;
- it is often quicker and cheaper to establish a standard time for a job.

Reflect and review

6 Answers to the quick quiz

Answer 1   The three transformation types were improving, caretaking and transferring.

Answer 2   The four resource types were people, capital, materials and information.

Answer 3   We defined efficiency as 'making the best use of resources, to achieve production of goods and services'.

Answer 4   One way of expressing this relationship is to say that, to be effective, an organization, individual or group has to achieve agreed objectives.

Answer 5   Quality can be defined as all the features and characteristics of a product or service which affect its ability to satisfy the needs of customers and users.

Answer 6   The dictionary definition is: 'an intangible asset taken into account in assessing the value of an enterprise, and reflecting its commercial reputation, customer connections, etc.' It is a capital resource.

Answer 7   Method study can be defined as: 'Systematically recording the way work is done, followed by analysis and development of the new methods, with the aim of doing the work better.'

Answer 8   We listed the steps of method study as: select, record, examine, develop, define and install, and maintain.

Answer 9   Flow process charts are used for this purpose.

Answer 10 A string diagram is used to determine the distance travelled by a person (or materials, equipment or information).

Answer 11 Work measurement is defined as the use of techniques to establish how long it takes a qualified worker to do a specified job to a defined level of performance.

Answer 12 Elements are short distinct tasks (such as tightening a screw, or moving an item from one location to another).

Answer 13 Allowed time is basic time + relaxation allowance + contingency or other allowances.

Answer 14 Predetermined motion time system (PMTS) identifies specific sets of basic human arm, leg or body motions, for which standard ratings can be applied. It eliminates the need for measuring the time taken for such movements in a job to be studied.

Answer 15 Benchmarking is a formal way of comparing a particular process in one organization against the best in the industry (or in the world), and using this knowledge as a basis for improvement.

Reflect and review

7 Certificate

Completion of this certificate by an authorized person shows that you have worked through all the parts of this workbook and satisfactorily completed the assessments. The certificate provides a record of what you have done that may be used for exemptions or as evidence of prior learning against other nationally certificated qualifications.

Pergamon Flexible Learning and NEBS Management are always keen to refine and improve their products. One of the key sources of information to help this process are people who have just used the product. If you have any information or views, good or bad, please pass these on.

NEBS MANAGEMENT DEVELOPMENT
SUPER SERIES
THIRD EDITION

Improving Efficiency

Dave Pearce

has satisfactorily completed this workbook

Name of signatory *Barbara Strudwick*

Position *Senior Training Consultant*

Signature *Barbara Strudwick*

Date *7 October 2003*

Official stamp

CORPORATE TRAINING & DEVELOPMENT
COUNTY HALL ANNEXE
COUNTY HALL
MARTINEAU LANE
NORWICH NR1 2UE

SUPER SERIES

SUPER SERIES 3
0-7506-3362-X   Full Set of Workbooks, User Guide and Support Guide

A. Managing Activities

0-7506-3295-X	1. Planning and Controlling Work
0-7506-3296-8	2. Understanding Quality
0-7506-3297-6	3. Achieving Quality
0-7506-3298-4	4. Caring for the Customer
0-7506-3299-2	5. Marketing and Selling
0-7506-3300-X	6. Managing a Safe Environment
0-7506-3301-8	7. Managing Lawfully - Health, Safety and Environment
0-7506-37064	8. Preventing Accidents
0-7506-3302-6	9. Leading Change
0-7506-4091-X	10. Auditing Quality

B. Managing Resources

0-7506-3303-4	1. Controlling Physical Resources
0-7506-3304-2	2. Improving Efficiency
0-7506-3305-0	3. Understanding Finance
0-7506-3306-9	4. Working with Budgets
0-7506-3307-7	5. Controlling Costs
0-7506-3308-5	6. Making a Financial Case
0-7506-4092-8	7. Managing Energy Efficiency

C. Managing People

0-7506-3309-3	1. How Organisations Work
0-7506-3310-7	2. Managing with Authority
0-7506-3311-5	3. Leading Your Team
0-7506-3312-3	4. Delegating Effectively
0-7506-3313-1	5. Working in Teams
0-7506-3314-X	6. Motivating People
0-7506-3315-8	7. Securing the Right People
0-7506-3316-6	8. Appraising Performance
0-7506-3317-4	9. Planning Training and Development
0-75063318-2	10. Delivering Training
0-7506-3320-4	11. Managing Lawfully - People and Employment
0-7506-3321-2	12. Commitment to Equality
0-7506-3322-0	13. Becoming More Effective
0-7506-3323-9	14. Managing Tough Times
0-7506-3324-7	15. Managing Time

D. Managing Information

0-7506-3325-5	1. Collecting Information
0-7506-3326-3	2. Storing and Retrieving Information
0-7506-3327-1	3. Information in Management
0-7506-3328-X	4. Communication in Management
0-7506-3329-8	5. Listening and Speaking
0-7506-3330-1	6. Communicating in Groups
0-7506-3331-X	7. Writing Effectively
0-7506-3332-8	8. Project and Report Writing
0-7506-3333-6	9. Making and Taking Decisions
0-7506-3334-4	10. Solving Problems

SUPER SERIES 3 USER GUIDE + SUPPORT GUIDE

0-7506-37056	1. User Guide
0-7506-37048	2. Support Guide

SUPER SERIES 3 CASSETTE TITLES

0-7506-3707-2	1. Complete Cassette Pack
0-7506-3711-0	2. Reaching Decisions
0-7506-3712-9	3. Making a Financial Case
0-7506-3710-2	4. Customers Count
0-7506-3709-9	5. Being the Best
0-7506-3708-0	6. Working Together

To Order - phone us direct for prices and availability details
(please quote ISBNs when ordering)
College orders: 01865 314333 • Account holders: 01865 314301
Individual purchases: 01865 314627 (please have credit card details ready)

We Need Your Views

We really need your views in order to make the Super Series 3 (SS3) an even better learning tool for you. Please take time out to complete and return this questionnaire to Marketing Department, Pergamon Flexible Learning, Linacre House, Jordan Hill, Oxford, OX2 8DP.

Name:..

Address:...

....

Title of workbook:..

If applicable, please state which qualification you are studying for. If not, please describe what study you are undertaking, and with which organisation or college:

....

Please grade the following out of 10 (10 being extremely good, 0 being extremely poor):

Content	....	Appropriateness to your position	....
Readability	....	Qualification coverage	....

What did you particularly like about this workbook?
....
....
....

Are there any features you disliked about this workbook? Please identify them.
....
....
....

Are there any errors we have missed? If so, please state page number: ....

How are you using the material? For example, as an open learning course, as a reference resource, as a training resource etc.
....

How did you hear about Super Series 3?:

Word of mouth: ☐   Through my tutor/trainer: ☐   Mailshot: ☐

Other (please give details):...
....

Many thanks for your help in returning this form.